348.73
HOUA

DATE DUE	
SEP 15 1995	
DEC 11 1995	
MAR 01 1996	
JUL 23 1998	
FEB 3 1999	

DEMCO, INC. 38-2971

THE
DEATH
OF
COMMON
SENSE

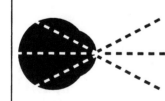

This Large Print Book carries the
Seal of Approval of N.A.V.H.

THE
DEATH
OF
COMMON
SENSE

How Law
Is Suffocating America

Philip K. Howard

G.K. Hall & Co.
Thorndike, Maine

Published in 1995 by arrangement with Random House, Inc.

G.K. Hall Large Print Core Collection.

The text of this Large Print edition is unabridged.
Other aspects of the book may vary from the original edition.

Set in 16 pt. News Plantin by Warren Doersam.

Printed in the United States on permanent paper.

Library of Congress Cataloging in Publication Data

Howard, Philip K.
    The death of common sense : how law is suffocating
America / Philip K. Howard.
        p.   cm.
    ISBN 0-7838-1361-9 (lg. print : hc)
    1. Law — United States. 2. Law reform — United States.
3. Bureaucracy — United States. 4. Common sense. I. Title.
KF384.H69   1995
349.73—dc20
[347.3]   95-13478

FOR OLIVIA, CHARLOTTE, LILY,
AND
ALEXANDER, AND FOR ALEXANDRA

CONTENTS

I

The Death of Common Sense

In the winter of 1988, nuns of the Missionaries of Charity were walking through the snow in the South Bronx in their saris and sandals to look for an abandoned building that they might convert into a homeless shelter. Mother Teresa, the Nobel Prize winner and head of the order, had agreed on the plan with Mayor Ed Koch after visiting him in the hospital several years earlier. The nuns came to two fire-gutted buildings on 148th Street and, finding a Madonna among the rubble, thought that perhaps providence itself had ordained the mission. New York City offered the abandoned buildings at one dollar each, and the Missionaries of Charity set aside $500,000 for the reconstruction. The nuns developed a plan to provide temporary care for sixty-four homeless men in a communal setting that included a dining room and kitchen on the first floor, a lounge on the second floor, and small dormitory rooms on the third and fourth floors. The only unusual thing about the plan was that Missionaries of Charity, in addition to their vow of poverty, avoid the routine use of modern conveniences. There would be no dishwashers or other appliances; laundry would be done by hand. For New York

City, the proposed homeless facility would be (literally) a godsend.

Although the city owned the buildings, no official had the authority to transfer them except through an extensive bureaucratic process. For a year and a half the nuns, wanting only to live a life of ascetic service, found themselves instead traveling in their sandals from hearing room to hearing room, presenting the details of the project and then discussing the details again at two higher levels of city government. In September 1989 the city finally approved the plan and the Missionaries of Charity began repairing the fire damage.

Providence, however, was no match for law. New York's building code, they were told after almost two years, requires an elevator in every new or renovated multiple-story building. The Missionaries of Charity explained that because of their beliefs they would never use the elevator, which also would add upward of $100,000 to the cost. The nuns were told the law could not be waived even if an elevator didn't make sense.

Mother Teresa gave up. She didn't want to devote that much extra money to something that wouldn't really help the poor: According to her representative, "The Sisters felt they could use the money much more usefully for soup and sandwiches." In a polite letter to the city expressing their regrets, the Missionaries of Charity noted that the episode "served to educate us about the law and its many complexities."

Law is generally thought of in its Perry Mason

sense, but courtroom dramas do not touch most of our lives. The law of government, on the other hand, controls almost every activity of common interest — fixing the pothole in front of the house, running public schools, regulating day care centers, controlling behavior in the workplace, cleaning up the environment, and deciding whether Mother Teresa gets a building permit.

No person decided to spite Mother Teresa. It was the law. And what it required offends common sense. There are probably 1 million buildings in New York without elevators. Homeless people would love to live in almost any one of these. Walking up a flight of stairs is not, after all, the greatest problem in their lives. But the law, aspiring to the perfect housing abode, has accumulated so many good ideas that the only type of new housing that is permitted must satisfy middle-class standards. A law that dictates either a model home or no home is probably fine for some, but what about those trying to provide housing for the poor?

Even serene suburban landscapes are stamped out of law's mold. Have you ever noticed how new housing subdivisions have an open, almost empty look? It isn't just the absence of trees. The streets are fifty feet wide, about 50 percent wider than streets were a few decades ago. Why? Because the traffic engineers who wrote the standard code after World War II believed that streets should be wide enough to allow two fire engines going in opposite directions to pass each other at 50 miles an hour. Andres Duany, a Miami architect who specializes in designing new towns, maintains that the traffic engineers have thereby depleted human interaction and fellowship from modern America. He calls them the "devils."

The two-fire-engine rule did not evolve because it was sensible or by amazing coincidence of judgment by town boards around the country. It was part of a model code that was accepted as "modern," and cities and towns fell before it like dominoes. Once the words were designated as law, there was no longer a need to think about it. Almost no one who builds new houses knows why the requirement is there. Nor do bureaucrats. They abide by it because they have to. It's the law.

John Marshall was an early chief justice of the Supreme Court, so it is fitting that the John Marshall Elementary School on Long Island should be perhaps the first primary school in America to recognize the legal hazards involved in children's art. Children's art, as we know, is usually made on paper. At the John Marshall Elementary School, as in every other school in America, children's art is tacked to the wall. Words and letters are also tacked up for the children to see. The law in New York, you may be surprised to learn, does not permit this, or at least not much of it. The state fire code actually addresses the public hazard explicitly: "[S]tudent art displays . . . [must be] kept at least two feet from ceilings, 10 feet from exits [which means any door] and . . . not exceed 20% of the wall surface."

The issue came up during a Halloween party in 1993. The local fire chief was there dressed as Officer MacGruff, "the police dog who promotes safety and drug awareness." As a diligent officer of the law, he noticed all the Halloween decorations and student art that had been attached to the walls. Within days, Officer MacGruff had done his duty. The school, according to one observer, now looked "about as inviting as a bomb shelter." All the art was gone. The school superintendent, having been accused of permitting a legal violation, suggested that he was aware of the law all along but had used a rule of thumb "on how much to decorate." Liz Skinner, a first grade teacher, was confused: "The essence of primary education is that children show pride in their work." No one had ever heard of fire caused by children's art, but there was a law just to make sure. So the art came down.

Amoco Oil Company needs no Officer MacGruff to tell it the law. It has regiments of lawyers. When the Environmental Protection Agency (EPA), after years of hearings, passed a rule requiring that specific equipment be put in smokestacks to filter benzene, a harmful pollutant, Amoco complied and spent $31 million at its Yorktown, Virginia, refinery. In 1989 a chance encounter on an airplane between James Lounsbury of EPA and Debora Sparks of Amoco led to a discussion about the frustrations and inadequacies of environmental law. One thing led to another and, with some trepidation, Amoco let a team from EPA into its Yorktown plant to see how the environmental rules, written in window-less rooms in Washington piled high with scientific evidence and legal briefs, actually worked in practice.

EPA found that its precisely drawn regulation almost totally missed the pollution. The Amoco refinery was emitting significant amounts of benzene, but nowhere near the smokestacks. The pollution was at the loading docks, where gasoline is pumped into barges. Just as fumes escape when you use an old-style nozzle when filling up your car at the gas station, large quantities of benzene were escaping as Amoco pumped several hundred million gallons of gasoline every year into barges. Once EPA and Amoco officials actually stood on the dock together and realized the problem, the solution was easy and relatively inexpensive. Meanwhile, pursuant to the rigid dictates of a thirty-five-page rule that many government experts had spent years fine-tuning, Amoco had spent $31 million to capture an insignificant amount of benzene at the smokestack. The rule was almost perfect in its failure: It maximized the cost to Amoco while minimizing the benefit to the public.

The Amoco incident brought to the surface a long-simmering suspicion that, in the words of EPA administrator Carol Browner, there are "really serious problems" with environmental regulation in this country. Environmental laws and rules, now seventeen volumes of fine print, often seem to miss the mark or prove counterproductive. Under one requirement, before industrial land with any toxic waste can be used, it must be cleaned up to almost perfect purity. It sounds great, but the effect is to drive industry out to virgin fields, where it encounters no such costs. Instead of cleaning up one dirty lot, the strict law creates a second dirty lot. Then, of course, jobs are moved away from cities, to places that workers can only reach by driving long distances, which causes yet more pollution. A final irony is that whoever cleaned the polluted land would often be required to incinerate it, literally burning tons of dirt, a process that itself generates significant pollution. Environmental laws have accomplished much, but not because the laws were generally sensible. Spending a trillion dollars in the last twenty years was bound to clean some things up, however inefficiently.

Big government is the usual suspect for these failures: If only government got out of our hair, many think, everything would work fine. But dreaming of an agrarian republic is not likely to help much. No one I know wants to eliminate environmental protection. Fire codes are a good idea; we wouldn't want the house next door built of kindling. The more important question is not why government is so big — we know in our hearts that any reduction would only occur at the edges — but why, with a few exceptions, it fails in even its simplest tasks. Government has imposed fire codes for centuries, but only our age has succeeded in barring children's art from school walls.

Politicians spend their lives apologizing for government. They all promise to fix it, but the slogans are so tired and the performance so dismal that the overall effect is more like propaganda. "A More Responsive Government" and "A New Age" are typical recent campaign slogans. Everyone wants to help. Universities and think tanks frequently put out excellent studies and ideas that Congress listens to with interest but rarely acts on. I always liked the idea of Robert Litan and William Nordhaus for a "regulatory budget": No law could be passed without a budget detailing its actual cost to society. Dan Osborne's and Ted Gaebler's *Reinventing Government* is filled with good ideas about government management, and Vice-President Al Gore and Massachusetts governor Bill Weld have picked up on them to try to improve government services. In the wake of the Amoco episode, EPA administrator Browner has suggested that Congress needs to give agencies greater leeway; another expert recently wrote a book arguing more or less the opposite, that Congress has to exercise more control over inept bureaucracies.

Most of these efforts seem to be bumping up against a larger problem. So far in my adult life nothing significant seems to have changed, except that government has become increasingly distant.

"The characteristic complaint of our time seems to be not that government provides no reasons," said former justice William Brennan, "but that its reasons often seem remote from human beings who must live with the consequences." Government acts like some extraterrestrial power, not an institution that exists to serve us. Its actions have an arbitrary quality: It almost never deals with real-life problems in a way that reflects an understanding of the situation.

Most people don't think about the connection between government and how law works. Government can't do anything except as law allows. We know Congress passes laws and authorizes bureaucracies to pass rules and regulations, but we focus mainly on what we want the law to do. Only a few specialists within the Beltway question how the laws and rules are implemented. And while these specialists debate numerous issues — for example, whether it is Congress or agencies that should establish the details of implementation — the one question they apparently almost never raise is whether the rules should be detailed.

Making rules as precise as possible has become almost a religious tenet. "Only precise, specific guidelines," said Herbert Kaufman, of the Brookings Institution, in 1977, "can assure common treatment of like cases." Otherwise, he said, "programs lose all consistency." As nearly as possible, another scholar wrote, legal rules should be "self-executing" and "aim toward solutions that can be carried into effect without discretionary administration." In 1970, during a lawmaking surge that began with Lyndon Johnson's Great Society, federal appeals judge J. Skelly Wright attacked the idea of administrators having freedom to make decisions as the "soft underbelly of the American legal system" and called on "all branches of government to join in the fight against discretion" by passing more rules: "An interlocking network of rules, laid out in advance, can serve as a bulwark which strengthens the agency and prevents co-option by the forces which it is attempting to regulate." Professor Kenneth Davis, the author of perhaps the most famous administrative law text, asserted that "[a]dministrative rule-making is . . . one of the greatest inventions of modern government." Through detailed rules, regulation would be made certain.

Certainty, we seem to think, is important to law. Of course it is, you are probably muttering under your breath. It is, after all, the law. But look up at what we've built: a legal colossus unprecedented in the history of civilization, with legal dictates numbering in the millions of words and growing larger every day. Our regulatory system has become an instruction manual. It tells us and bureaucrats exactly what to do and how to do it. Detailed rule after detailed rule addresses every eventuality, or at least every situation lawmakers and bureaucrats can think of. Is it a coincidence that almost every encounter with government is an exercise in frustration?

This system is not some constitutional mandate

(although most people treat it with that kind of reverence) but a comparatively recent invention. Only three decades ago, in the 1960s, government puttered along without detailed rules to meet every eventuality. Forest rangers, as Al Gore has noted, could carry the list of rules in their shirt pockets. They did just fine armed with a pamphlet of rules and their own common sense. Now they have to consult several volumes of fine print.

It is not hard to imagine a world in which New York City could easily accommodate the Missionaries of Charity in their preference not to use elevators. No spasms of fear would overtake most principals or fire marshals called upon to take the risk, if it can be called such, of having children's art on the walls. One can even imagine that Amoco, instead of dutifully (and at great expense) trying to comply with thousands of pages of awkward legal requirements, might prefer to sit down with environmental regulators and negotiate a pollution-control plan.

But that is not the way we have constructed our modern legal system. We seem to have achieved the worst of both worlds: a system of regulation that goes too far while it also does too little.

This paradox is explained by the absence of the one indispensable ingredient of any successful human endeavor: use of judgment. In the decades since World War II, we have constructed a system of regulatory law that basically outlaws common sense. Modern law, in an effort to be "self-executing," has shut out our humanity.

The motives were logical enough: Specific legal mandates would keep government in close check and provide crisp guidelines for private citizens. But it doesn't work. Human activity can't be regulated without judgment by humans.

BLINDED BY CERTAINTY

The safety of every worker "to the maximum extent feasible" was the goal of Congress when it passed the Occupational Health and Safety Act in 1970. A new department, the Occupational Safety and Health Administration (OSHA), was formed within the Department of Labor to pass safety regulations and to inspect workplaces. For twenty-five years OSHA has been hard at work. The agency has over 4,000 detailed regulations, dictating everything from the height of railings (42 inches) to how much a plank can stick out from a temporary scaffold (no more than 12 inches). There are about 2,000 safety inspectors in the field, not many compared with 6 million workplaces, but enough to do some good if they focus on firms with bad safety records. Several hundred billion dollars have been spent by industry to comply with OSHA's rules. Intuitively, all this expense must have done some good.

It hasn't. Safety in the American workplace is about the same as it was in 1970. A tour through the Glen-Gery brick factory, near Reading, Pennsylvania, gives an indication why.

Brick making is not generally considered hazardous. People have been doing it more or less the same way for several thousand years. Brick makers mix clay and water, apply heat, and then stack up the finished bricks for delivery. Over the millennia, no hidden hazards have ever been identified with brick making, no "red-clay disease" or the like. But modern brick makers use an assembly line to mass-produce them, so there are machines and kilns to exercise caution around, and almost all machinery holds the potential for accidents.

OSHA inspectors visit the Glen-Gery factory once or twice a year. The inspectors walk around the factory with a measuring tape and always find violations. They are especially interested in railings. Glen-Gery has been cited for having railings 39 and 40 inches high, not the regulation 42 inches, in older parts of the factory. In one area already partitioned off by railings, OSHA required several thousand dollars to be spent for an automatic shutoff on a one-foot-wide conveyer belt. The rule applied, OSHA pointed out, because occasionally a repairman might enter the area and step across it.

Warnings are posted everywhere. A large POISON sign dominates one side of a storage shed filled with bags of something hazardous: It turns out to be sand. OSHA categorizes sand as poison because sand, including the beach sand you and I sunbathe on in blissful ignorance, contains a mineral called silica. Some scientists believe that silica, in conditions found nowhere except in certain grinding and mining operations, might cause cancer.

During an inspection several years ago, an OSHA inspector noted that a worker wearing a dust mask had a beard, violating a rule that requires a close fit between face and mask. The dust was not heavy or of hazardous content, and, even when used over a beard, the mask filtered out most of what there was. But the rule was clear and, like most rules, did not distinguish among different situations. Nor did it matter that the worker was Amish and faced the choice of abrogating his religious convictions by shaving his beard or quitting. He quit.

If the inspectors can't find anything else, they go to the factory shop, where machinery is fixed. There are always some oil rags used to wipe down gears and clean bearings that can be cited as a fire hazard. The inspectors also spend a lot of time upstairs in the office looking at paperwork; Glen-Gery was recently cited because the wrong box was accidentally checked on some internal form. About 50 percent of all OSHA violations across the nation are for not keeping the forms correctly.

Bob Hrasok, Glen-Gery's full-time manager in charge of regulatory compliance, considers each inspection a kind of negative lottery: "Every inspector knows different rules," and will always find a violation, even though "we have done basically everything they asked for the last twenty years." "Everything they say is not wrong," says Ron Smeal, the plant manager, "but most of the requirements miss the point." The changes that really irk Smeal are the ones forcing workers to change habits that have been successful and accident-free. "Doing it a new way after years of doing it the old way," Smeal notes, "is just an invitation for an accident."

The one thing of no interest to the inspectors is Glen-Gery's safety record. In the inevitable discussion after each inspection, they are unwilling even to discuss whether a violation actually has anything to do with safety. Glen-Gery has never had an incident, for example, related to its railings. OSHA inspectors, in the words of everyone who has to deal with them, are "just traffic cops" looking for rule violations.

OSHA's head office is no better. Glen-Gery once tried to ask for an interpretation of a rule before changing part of the plant and, after going through several levels of the OSHA bureaucracy, struck out. No one at OSHA, at least not anyone Glen-Gery could find, was allowed to venture an opinion about safety.

It is not surprising that, as with the rest of American industry, Glen-Gery's safety was not improved by all the money it spent complying with OSHA.

Since 1988, however, Glen-Gery's safety record has improved dramatically. When Ron Smeal became manager, he calculated that the company was losing over $30,000 per injury in health and unemployment benefit costs. He got together with some key supervisors and they decided to institute safety contests. At the end of each quarter, prizes like tool sets are given to each worker who has not lost a workday. This seems to have had a good effect and has been expanded to all Glen-Gery plants. Recently, the company stepped up the campaign and started distributing a tax-free cash sum by lottery at the end of each quarter: The lower the overall injury record, the higher the award. These contests, intended to instill peer-group pressure to be careful, have worked almost like magic: The number of workdays lost has declined by 75 percent. Creating a culture of safety has worked where all OSHA's rules did not.

OSHA's false premise, according to Bob Hrasok, is its fixation with physical conditions and paperwork. Five out of six accidents, he points out, are caused by human error. Hrasok thinks that "trying to make everything idiot-proof" is itself dangerous: "Workers don't have to think, and bosses get tied down with nit-picking regulations."

It is as if OSHA's goal, the safety of workers, is obscured from view by all the rules intended to advance it. In a culture of legal precision, law-makers focus on what they can write a clear rule about. Solid, objective rules, like the precise height of railings, satisfy lawmakers' longing for certainty. Human activity, however, cannot be so neatly categorized. The more precise the rule, the less sensible law seems to be.

On the banks of the Mississippi River in Minneapolis, a mountain of 75,000 tons of lime sludge slowly built up over sixty years, the by-product of a gas-acetylene plant. By the early 1980s, something had to be done with it: It sat directly in the path of a proposed highway. The mountain was, by most accounts, harmless. Lime, which is highly alkaline, is used in agriculture and pollution control to lower the acidity of land and water. EPA and Minnesota's pollution-control agency, however, each has a rule that designates as "hazardous waste" any material with a pH of over 12.5. The rule generally makes sense, but not for lime; the pH is also affected by dampness, and the mountain of lime sludge had a pH of 12.7.

Faced with this conflict between law and reality, the Minnesota pollution board then did what I understand is a typical test in this age of high technology: It got a rabbit, shaved a spot on its back, and applied the hazardous waste. Nothing bad happened, you may be relieved to hear, and the pollution board was prepared to sneak by the rule. But a disgruntled contractor who had lost the bid for removing the lime went public with the fact that the lime was, at least in the eyes of the law, "hazardous waste." The highway was stopped dead in its tracks.

The state got another idea: A local power plant wanted to use the lime in its pollution-control efforts. But the power plant would take it only if it didn't come with the tag of hazardous waste, which, under environmental laws, would be like agreeing to a criminal conviction. Unfortunately, even though everyone knew the lime wasn't hazardous and the purpose was to decrease other forms of pollution, the rule was crystal clear on this point; the rule even had a separate prohibition against waiving anything that qualified as "hazardous waste." Minnesota's Pollution Control Agency could not provide the comfort. The lime was finally pushed to the side onto adjoining parkland, where, with the help of the sun, it eventually dried its way into lawfulness.

Great wisdom is not the common trait of most lawmakers, but even if it were, they still would not be able to anticipate every future contingency. Indeed, language itself is too imperfect. Legal philosopher H.L.A. Hart has noted that "in all fields of experience, not only that of rules, there is a limit, inherent in the nature of language, to the guidance" that words can provide.

Consider, for example, trying to write a rule for a safe hammer. Design is important. So is the quality of materials. But even with good design and materials, it could be assembled in a shoddy way. How often the hammer is used is also relevant. So is whether it is used in the damp climate of Seattle or the dry heat of Phoenix. How the hammer will be taken care of is important — whether it gets tossed in the back of the pickup truck day after day or sits in a drawer. What the hammer is used for is critical — tapping tacks into the wall of an art gallery, or banging twelve-penny nails through two-by-fours. Very important, of course, is the skill of the user.

Specifying a safe hammer, a simple-sounding task, is beyond the capacity of a bundle of words. There can be "grades" of hammers, but which grade is appropriate will require the exercise of judgment by someone. So will assessing whether the hammer has been weakened by use. To make sense, even the simplest rules require judgment: A 55 mph speed limit should be waived for someone rushing to the hospital. Context is vital in law, as it is in life. Modern law, however, presses as hard as it can to cover every eventuality.

Often, the ink is barely dry when the precise requirements begin to subvert the law's purpose. Several years ago, the Federal Aviation Administration (FAA) passed a rule authorizing a "head tax" on departing passengers to help fund mass transit to airports. The writer of the rule, trying to clarify every eventuality, wanted to make sure no city used this airport tax to subsidize regular commuter transit. The rule thus requires an "exclusive" system and prohibits any "facility shared with other mass transit."

New York was the perfect candidate for the FAA program: Crawling in New York traffic to catch a flight at JFK is the very definition of stress. A system in New York could also get high ridership: Unlike most sprawling cities, New York retains a dominant center-city hub that generates much of the passenger volume. Because of the way the rule is written, however, New York City can't link its airport transport into the tracks to Penn Station and Grand Central Station, exactly where it makes the most sense. Those tracks would not be "exclusive" as required by the rule. The rule writer, aware that most cities have no rail infrastructure, probably didn't even think of New York.

The law thus prohibits the only sensible program for New York. What is most remarkable, however, is that New York, instead of pounding the table to get the rule changed, meekly accepts it. The rule, after all, is quite clear.

Taking the words of law seriously, particularly the pseudo-technical drivel that pours out, is itself a pathology. It is not hard to imagine a world in which an inspector says, "Oh, that railing looks fine," or the FAA administrator looks over a proposed airport transit system to make sure there is no subsidy of local commuters. Instead, the words are glared at in a vacuum that only lawyers and bureaucrats are able to take seriously. That is part of the modern legal ethos: The words of law will tell us exactly what to do. Judgment is foreclosed not simply by the language of the words. It is also foreclosed by the belief that judgment has no place in the application of law.

The president of Italy learned about this peculiar attitude toward American law when, at the end of a visit to Washington in the late 1980s, he invited a senior U.S. official to accompany him back on his chartered plane. A better diplomatic opportunity for the U.S. official would be difficult to imagine: eight hours with the president of an important country. The State Department said no, however, citing a rule that prohibits taking anything of value from a foreign country. No more than two seconds is required to understand why, at least in that situation, the rule made no sense: The official was not being personally enriched. The taxpayers, after all, were going to pay for his trip back. But the language of the rule, viewed in the abstract, seemed to apply. After an internal battle State Department lawyers relented. But the official had to give the Italian government a plane ticket that could be cashed in for reimbursement.

How peculiar the episode must have seemed to the Italians. A free plane ride to Sardinia for a luxury weekend, on the other hand, might well have been inappropriate. As with most things, circumstances are critical. The lawyers instead focused on the legal language as if it were the oracle, and refused to act without its clear permission.

Managing the pollution and poisons of modern society may be where detail gets in the way the most. Lead poisoning, for example, can be very serious for children. Because lead-based paint was in common usage before it was banned in 1978, many old houses have lead on their walls. Scraping away lead paint can be a messy process, however, and can make the problem much worse. Getting rid of lead paint may be the best course in some situations; in others it might be better to leave well enough alone. Judgment is required. But the law in many states doesn't permit judgment. In Massachusetts, for example, the lead paint must be removed (or "abated") in any household where there is a child under the age of six; no exceptions are permitted. Horrible stories of children's blood-lead levels worsening after abatement began to appear in the press; one parent said her child woke up screaming with nightmares for months following the extensive injections required to treat high lead levels caused by the abatement process. But the law requires it, even where there is no evidence of lead poisoning — ostensibly, to save small children.

The Manhattan Institute's Richard Miniter tells the saga of Tony Benjamin, the father of eight, who, after reading about lead poisoning, made the mistake of looking to the government for help. He had his children tested and found that the youngest had lead levels almost at the danger threshold. He then got a lead detection kit and, as is common in old houses, found lead beneath the surface of his walls. He called a state official, who said not to worry because Mr. Benjamin had recently painted over the old coats.

But his child's test results had been filed with the city health department. One day, unannounced, the city inspectors arrived. They stamped VIOLATION in red ink on every nick in his paint and, after finding seventeen nicks, declared the house a health hazard. Mr. Benjamin was told to move his family out of their home and strip and repaint it in large sections. If he failed to comply immediately, he was told, he could be fined over $8,000.

Mr. Benjamin couldn't afford to do what the inspectors demanded. Certainly, he couldn't vacate his home with his eight children. Where would they go? Meanwhile, the youngest child's lead level had dropped well below a level considered dangerous. But the law still required abatement, clearly and without exception. The inspectors, who kept returning impatiently, said that the child's lead levels "were irrelevant and that they just wanted him to comply with the rules."

Vaclav Havel, the president of the Czech Republic and a playwright, is also a noted observer of the modern world order. He has observed that in a communist society people were not allowed to act without explicit authorization. In a free society, by contrast, the presumption is the opposite: We are free to do what we want unless it is prohibited. The idea that highly detailed rules will tell us exactly what to do changes the presumption back again: We can't do what we want because the law details our course. It does not matter if Mr. Benjamin's home is doing no harm. The rules require lead paint abatement. It does not matter if the purpose of the FAA rule is served by linking New York airports to a train station. The words say something different.

Governing by excruciating detail, dictating every result in advance, might indeed suggest to you the pattern with which Mr. Havel has so much experience. Modern regulatory law resembles central planning. Instead of an economist in Moscow making complex flowcharts on how to harvest Siberia's wheat, generally forgetting something like spare parts for delivery trucks, we have highly detailed laws and rules, often written years earlier, that catalog the conditions for our action. While in Siberia bumper crops of wheat rotted for want of delivery trucks, in our own country Mother Teresa is not able to build a homeless shelter and benzene escapes needlessly into the air while millions are spent trying to catch it in the wrong place. The failing is the same: Rigidity of legal dictates precludes the exercise of judgment at the time and place of the activity.

Government in both cases is blinded by its own predetermined rules, entranced by the rationalists' promise that all can be set out before we get there. As the philosopher Michael Oakeschott observed, "The Rationalist . . . does not merely neglect the kind of knowledge which would save him, he begins by destroying it. First he turns out the light and then complains that he cannot see."

There are differences, of course. The Soviets tried to run their country like a puppeteer pulling millions of strings. In our country, the words of law are like millions of trip wires, preventing us from doing the sensible thing.

The unfortunate resemblance to central planning, someone could argue, might be the necessary cost for a legal system that is certain and fair. But the tradition of American law, generally thought to be fairer than the Soviets', is based on an entirely different philosophy. As we rebuilt government in the second half of the twentieth century, we almost completely ignored the strains underlying our most hallowed legal traditions.

How Law Replaced Humanity

The tension between legal certainty and life's complexities was a primary concern of those who built our legal system. The Constitution is a model of flexible law that can evolve with changing times and unforeseen circumstances. This remarkable document, shorter than EPA's benzene rules, gave us three branches of government and a Bill of Rights built on vague principles like "due process."

How detailed the Constitution should be was a matter of importance to the drafters. Alexander Hamilton, for example, argued that the Bill of Rights was too specific. Enumerating any rights at all, he argued, would imply the absence of other rights. Today, we no longer remember that specificity is even an issue, or that words can impose rigidity as well as offer clarity.

What is known as the "common law," which we inherited from England, still governs relations among citizens. For centuries before the rise of the modern state and all its statutes and rules, the common law dominated the legal landscape; its principles still provide the framework of our legal system. The common law is not a legislative enactment but the synthesis of general standards derived from countless court decisions. We must drive our cars reasonably, for example, or else be accountable to those we injure.

The common law is the opposite of ironclad rules that seek to predetermine results. Application of the common law always depends on the circumstances: The accident caused by swerving to avoid the child is excusable; falling asleep at the wheel is not. The most important standard is what a reasonable person would have done. Every principle has exceptions. More than anything else, the common law glorifies the particular situation and invites common sense. It was the common law that developed the jury system, in which a group of peers, not an expert in law, would decide right and wrong in each case. Since it grows with every new court decision, the common law also evolves with changing times. Justice Benjamin Cardozo, considered the greatest common law judge of this century, said in the 1920s that the common law "is at bottom the philosophy of pragmatism. Its truth is relative, not absolute."

The American legal community, like other professions, has occasionally shown a tendency to overlook the obvious. As remarkable as it seems today, lawyers once believed that the common law provided certainty, that the one true result would emerge if they stared long enough at all the cases or the principles synthesized in Lord Blackstone's common law treatise. Since opposing lawyers typically took diametrically opposed positions, often with great conviction, one would think a little self-doubt as to law's certainty might have crept in. But no. Law, like the Bible, was certain.

With the Constitution guaranteeing freedom and the common law guaranteeing justice, we have long taken pride that America is a "government of laws, not of men."

Law had an identity crisis when Oliver Wendell Holmes, Jr., then a Harvard law professor, suggested in 1881 that law was not certain after all but depended on how the judge and jury saw the facts: "General propositions do not decide concrete cases." When the law was exposed for its naked uncertainty, the shock stimulated a wide range of reform movements. Some reformers wanted to accelerate the codification of the common law into statutes; a related movement looked to turn law into a science; the legal "realists" advocated everything, including turning law into a branch of psychiatry. The most famous description of the new realism was by Professor Robert Hutchins: "What a judge has for breakfast is more important than any principle of law."

To suggest there was an overreaction is to spare you the migraine of four decades of intellectual spasms in which famous scholars reversed their positions every other year. Holmes himself did not understand all the excitement. He, like most lawyers today, looked to judges only to be impartial and competent, not omnipotent. Probably the most fruitful development out of the confusion was the founding, in 1923, of the American Law Institute, which compiled the common law principles in a series of books, called the "Restatement of the Laws." Although "legal certainty [was] the institute's only objective," important principles like "reasonableness" and "good faith" look as uncertain in Restatement print as they sound in closing arguments. The Restatement, which basically modernized Blackstone's treatise, remains the repository of American common law.

For our nation's first century, statutory law was used mainly to allocate money for defense and public works. Statutes began to replace the common law in importance at the turn of the century, when the Progressive movement began to try to bust industrial trusts and curb exploitation of child labor.

With the New Deal, statutes began to dominate the legal landscape, providing job relief, welfare programs, and Social Security; agencies like the Securities and Exchange Commission were created as part of a broad plan to regulate the economy. In a nod toward the age of science, these statutes were written with greater specificity than before; Arthur Dean, one of the drafters of the securities laws, used to remind me almost daily how certain provisions are interlocked perfectly. But the overall approach retained the practical philosophy of the common law. According to a 1937 report on administration to President Roosevelt:

> Government is a human institution. . . .
> It is human throughout; it rests not only
> on formal arrangements . . . but even more
> upon attitudes. . . . It is certainly not a
> machine. . . . What we want is not a stream-
> lined, chromium-trimmed government that
> looks well in the advertisement, but one that
> will actually deliver the goods in practice.

Lawmaking momentum was interrupted by World War II. But it surged again in the 1960s, providing social programs like Medicare, oversight in areas like worker safety, and control over common resources such as the environment. In the twenty years beginning with John F. Kennedy's administration, the number of federal agencies doubled.

Much of the growth in law, however, was due not to government's expanded role but to its techniques. We changed our attitude toward legal detail: The words of law expanded far faster than the new areas of law. The Federal Register, a daily report of new and proposed regulations, increased from 15,000 pages in the final year of John F. Kennedy's presidency to over 70,000 pages in the last year of George Bush's. The Interstate Highway System, still the country's largest postwar public works program, was authorized by a 1956 statute that ran 28 pages. A transportation act passed by Congress in 1991, which almost none of you probably noticed, was ten times longer. Today's local fire and building codes have roughly the same purposes as those of forty years ago, but are much longer.

As government took on an expanded role, legal draftsmen seemed to assume that law should be modernized as well. In the age of NASA, we would make law scientific. Highly specific and "self-executing" rules would cover every eventuality, preserve uniformity, and avoid discretion and possible abuse by officials. It sounded great, and everyone went for it. OSHA at one point had 140 regulations on wooden ladders, including one specifying the grain of the wood.

While lawmakers and bureaucrats demonstrated their energy in making laws, they showed no facility for paring them back. Most of these new legal dictates were stacked on top of the prior year's laws and rules. The agencies created by Congress have multiplied these statutory dictates, like fishes and loaves, into many more thousands of rules and regulations. EPA alone has over 10,000 pages of regulations. The result, after several decades of unrestrained growth, is a mammoth legal edifice unparalleled in history: Federal statutes and formal rules now total about 100 million words.

This trend toward legal detail was not confined to government. Business agreements in the United States now run to several hundred pages of single-spaced typing as the parties try to contemplate and negotiate every eventuality. In Switzerland, the same agreements would typically be documented in ten to twenty pages. When working on a contract, one lawyer received a proposed definition of the words *and/or* that was over three hundred words in length.

Human nature seems to lead people, or at least certain kinds of people, down this path. Bayless Manning, former dean of Stanford Law School, described the urge of "every expert" to elaborate and "exorcise the demon of ambiguity":

> With the best and purest of professional motives, we invariably propose elaboration as the answer to any problem . . . we relish the challenge to erect elegant logical structures that will "solve" the problem.

Once the idea is to cover every situation explicitly, the words of law expand like floodwaters that have broken through a dike. Rules elaborate on prior rules; detail breeds greater detail. There is no logical stopping point in the quest for certainty. If "loading" includes "filling," as EPA's benzene rule for some reason explicitly provides, then what is "filling"?

As laws began to pile up, there were a few cries in the dark. Louis Jaffe, a young intellectual of the New Deal who went on to be a distinguished professor of administrative law at Harvard, began to have second thoughts as early as the 1950s about what his generation was doing:

"We have too easily succumbed to the siren song of regulation or rather . . . of comprehensive regulation. We [are] too easily moved by notions of rationalized completeness." In 1982, Bayless Manning called for "radical simplification" of law. Since Manning's lonely plea, the words of law have increased again by a third.

Lawmakers in the 1960s probably didn't spend much time discussing intellectual history, but their approach can be traced back through currents of history to the seventeenth century. Making a system of laws where all is set forth precisely, each situation covered in advance, comes directly out of the Enlightenment. The philosophy of rationalism held that relations between citizens and state would be predetermined in advance, that a natural order in government could be found similar to the order that Isaac Newton thought he had found in nature.

The credo of this rationalistic order, like our law today, was that government should be self-executing and dispassionate. The idea spawned numerous reform movements, including socialism. It also led to the invention of modern bureaucracy, whose philosophy and tendencies were analyzed by the German sociologist Max Weber at the turn of the twentieth century: "Bureaucracy develops the more perfectly, the more it is 'dehumanized.' . . . [T]he professional bureaucrat . . . is only a small cog in a ceaselessly moving mechanism which prescribes to him an essentially fixed route of march."

The tradition of common law, where circumstances are critical, could hardly have been more different. Rationalism was anathema to the American spirit, which glorified individualism and the frontier, not regularity and sameness. In America, too much thinking was suspect. In 1856, for example, Congress passed a law that provided funding for consular officials "well-grounded in history, international law and the American Constitution." The next year it was repealed: "The best foreign consuls [are] backwoodsmen," a majority of Congressmen concluded, with "none of the education."

But it is a particularly American trait, as we all know, to take an idea and push it as hard as possible. When we made the switch to an activist government in the New Deal, and then to the modern regulatory state beginning in the 1960s, we did so with the gusto of pioneers blazing through the frontier. A new system of law that was made up of millions of words of new legal dictates, although antithetical to a system of law based on flexible principles, was embraced by us as a symbol of success.

Our bureaucracy is now organized with vastly more detail than those in Europe, which first embraced the philosophy of rationalism. Ours is bigger and better than anyone's. Rationalism in our country is now super-rationalism.

A few federal agencies still manage with nothing more than general mandates. The Federal Reserve Board sets monetary policy with virtually no constraints. The Comptroller of the Currency certifies banks as healthy based on standards like "safety and soundness." They look at each situation in context, and are considered highly effective. But these are the exceptions.

Critics of modern law and government pick out symptoms of ineptness and call for broad reforms. By and large, however, they continue to champion the idea that law should be as specific as possible. Walter Olson, an advocate of judicial reform and author of the influential 1991 book *The Litigation Explosion,* pondered whether litigation might decrease as "big rules give way to smaller, finer rules" and we enter "an era of clearer law." City planner Andres Duany, while exposing the anti-human effects of zoning codes, has called for more detailed codes to set everything straight. Theodore Lowi, in *The End of Liberalism,* in 1979, saw greater specificity as the antidote for special interest groups. There would be nothing for them to fight over, Lowi thought, if only law were clearer.

To most experts, the highest art of American lawmaking is precision. Only with precision can law achieve a scientific certainty. By the crafting of words, lawmakers will anticipate every situation, every exception. With obligations set forth precisely, everyone will know where they stand. Truth emerges in the crucible of the democratic process, and legal experts use their logic to transform it into a detailed guide for action. The greater the specificity, the more certain we are that we are providing a government of laws, not of men.

THE SLIDE FROM CERTAINTY TO IGNORANCE

Making law detailed, the theory goes, permits it to act as a clear guide. People will know exactly what is required. But modern law is unknowable. It is too detailed. Manuals for policemen in big cities often run over a thousand pages, and as if this weren't difficult enough, the police are supposed to comprehend ever-shifting constitutional constraints on the catching of criminals.

How can law function as a guide to action if almost no one knows it? Bob Hrasok believes that nobody, including the OSHA inspectors, knows all the OSHA regulations: "How can anybody know the fine print in four thousand rules?"

The drive for certainty has destroyed, not enhanced, law's ability to act as a guide. All you have to do is pick up any volume of the Code of Federal Regulations to confirm the truth of Bayless Manning's observation that "regulation has become so elaborate and technical that it is beyond the understanding of all but a handful of Mandarins." Indeed, if the tax code is already "beyond the capacity of the great majority of tax experts," as one prominent bar committee concluded, how are companies supposed to do the right thing?

The situation is almost hopeless for people trying to make it on their own. Dutch Noteboom, seventy-two, has owned a small meat-packing plant in Springfield, Oregon, for thirty-three years. The U.S. Department of Agriculture (USDA) has one full-time inspector on the premises, and another spends over half his time there. This level of regulatory attention is somewhat surprising, since Mr. Noteboom has only four employees. But the rules require that there be at least one inspector whenever livestock is slaughtered. Every day the inspectors sit there, "mainly talking on the phone," but they always find time to cite him for a violation. One citation was for "loose paint located twenty feet from any animal." Mr. Noteboom says, "I am swimming in paperwork," but "I don't even know a tenth" of the rules: "You should see all these USDA manuals."

Most small businesses don't suffer Mr. Noteboom's regulatory incarceration, but they don't know the law either. Several million small employers operate pursuant to their own moral code, comfortable only in the assurance that they could never figure out the letter of the law if they tried. This is a predicament one witness before Congress termed the syndrome of "involuntary noncompliance."

Dutch Noteboom just does his job as best as he can, relying on fifty-two years of experience, and endures daily humiliation at the hands of two inspectors who have nothing better to do than find rules that are violated. What good, we might ask ourselves, is a legal system that cannot be known?

From Protector to Protection Racket

Law that is perfectly clear, even if nearly impossible to know, should at least prevent government bureaucrats from exercising arbitrary authority. If some petty tyrant tries to get us, we can hire a lawyer, who will be able to find a protective rule somewhere.

This idea, perfectly logical, is also upside down. All the words of law certainly constrain the bureaucrats and, as we have seen, prevent them from doing the sensible thing: The Minnesota pollution-control people couldn't "un-designate" the lime mountain whose pH level qualified as hazardous. The detail narrows the regulator's jurisdiction but leaves ample room for meanness or abuse. If you need something, there is almost always room for him to say no. At the edges of the words there are always interpretations — for example, whether the plane ride from the Italian president was a personal benefit — that make it possible for the regulator to deny your request.

Looming over us is a larger, more troubling paradox: The quest for protection through certainty results in arbitrary power. How many people do you think comply with all the requirements of EPA or OSHA? OSHA itself has estimated that 80 percent of workplaces are not in compliance with the law. It has to be true that no one is in full compliance: Even on paper an accountant couldn't comply with four thousand rules. Is your supply closet neatly organized so that everything is "stable and secure," as required by Section 1910.176(b)? Have you checked recently? One observer has noted that it is common knowledge in the meat-packing industry, "denied only by USDA spokesmen, that if all meat-inspecting regulations were enforced to the letter, no meat-processor in America would be open for business."

Avoiding arbitrary authority is a wonderful idea. Instead, we have handed it out: When laws cannot be complied with, individual officials, who supposedly have no discretion, have complete power. Why do you think lawyers, who more often act like assassins, are generally so polite when they go down to the SEC or some other government agency? Because they know that no matter how precise the rules, the regulators can find a way to do them in.

Abuses occur every day. Under the Resource Conservation and Recovery Act, RCRA (called Rickra), a company that receives containers of hazardous material, including many common chemicals, must keep track of when each one is received and must then dispose of the material. This is hard but manageable. RCRA also requires, however, a ledger showing exactly where each container is located on the premises. Even large companies with separate environmental staffs can't accurately keep paperwork on exactly where each barrel is at any given moment within the plant. Tom Jorling, until recently commissioner of New York State's Department of Environmental Protection, views the enforcement of regulations like this as "a kind of extortion." He describes situations where federal environmental agents, whom he refers to as the "RCRA police," went into large companies that could not possibly maintain perfect paperwork for thousands of barrels, and then threatened a criminal indictment unless the company paid a large fine.

A colleague of mine and his wife worked hard for several years to renovate the bathrooms and kitchen of their Brooklyn brownstone. All plans were duly filed. Inspectors came periodically to see the work. They finally finished, got sign-offs from the inspectors, and went to get the certificate of occupancy. It was refused on the grounds that they had been living in the home. Of course, they had been living there; it is, after all, their home. But, they were told, the law prohibits "habitation" in a dwelling under renovation. No inspector, in all their visits, had ever told them of the rule. The rule itself suffered the typical defects of specificity. The language can't distinguish between a gutted home, which probably would not be appropriate to live in, and one being spruced up by the family living there. But that didn't matter to the bureaucrat at the desk. My colleague had broken the rule. It took him and his wife months (and another story) to get the problem straightened out.

Most bureaucrats presumably are not in a power game. Look at it from their point of view. They're put in the position of having to ignore the rules to allow an ordinary renovation or, indeed, to put meat on our tables. Only the paradox is perfect: If noncompliance can be found under any law, what protection do we think all this legal detail is providing?

THE UNFAIRNESS OF UNIFORMITY

Precision, the experts say, ensures fairness. By eliminating any room for judgment or discretion, law will be the same for everyone. Fairness, we all could agree, is indispensable to law. Fairness, however, is a far more subtle concept than making all the words on the page apply to everyone. Uniformity in law is not uniformity in effect.

In 1979 EPA passed a rule that required scrubbers to be placed in the smokestacks of every coal-burning power plant. The object was to minimize pollution. The same rule applied to every power plant across the country. It was perfectly uniform, and as everyone knew, the main purpose of the so-called uniform law was to subsidize eastern coal. The black coal mined in Appalachia burns dirty and, even with a scrubber, produces more pollution than the clean-burning brown coal mined in the West. Addressing coal pollution by requiring a scrubber forced western power plants to be dramatically cleaner than eastern plants, and eliminated altogether the incentive for eastern plants to buy cleaner western coal. The overall effect was a higher pollution level than necessary and extra costs of $4 billion.

Uniformity in the common law, consisting of broad principles like the "reasonable person" standard, generally permits adjustment for the circumstances. This type of uniform principle is almost synonymous with fairness. Uniform application of a detailed rule, on the other hand, will almost always favor one group over another.

Upper New York State has a tradition of bed and breakfasts, tourist lodgings managed by families in old farmhouses. The countryside is historic, the rates are attractive (often in the range of forty dollars per night), and the tourists get to spend the evening in front of a fireplace enjoying the lore of the area and making new friends. Virtually every one of these bed and breakfasts is operated illegally: Most cannot comply with fire codes specifying enclosed fire stairs and other requirements for "multistory transient lodging." Barring a last-minute legislative change, all of them will be shut down. A motel on the interstate (a one-story structure, not needing a fire escape) will pick up their business. Wouldn't you prefer to have a choice?

Uniformity turns out to be a loaded concept. Enclosed fire stairs are obviously important for a twenty-story hotel, and the cost is relatively small. For a two-story rooming house, the need is questionable and the cost is crippling.

Universal requirements that leave no room for judgment are almost never fair, even when the sole point is to assure fairness. In 1973, a prominent New York lawyer and former judge, Marvin Frankel, had the idea that criminal sentences suffered from too much variation. He certainly had a point: There were stories of different judges imposing sentences ranging from nothing to twenty years for the same crime. His idea developed momentum, and a "sentencing commission" was established. The commission ultimately created a 258-box matrix from which federal courts had to calculate all jail sentences. Judges are now permitted only minimal leeway.

All the components of the sentencing grid — whether it was first offense, whether a weapon was used, how many drugs were sold — are the best that our smartest legal minds could come up with. All the judges would have to do is calculate the points. At last, many believed, we had created a fair and uniform way of treating criminal defendants. It all sounded perfect.

Most who use it — judges, lawyers, prosecutors — consider it a disaster. The sentence for a drug conviction, for example, increases with the quantity of drugs involved, measured by weight. Some lower-level thug driving a delivery truck, who probably did not know how much he was delivering, gets a life sentence, while a pusher who sells heroin to a child gets two years. The jail time for selling the same amount of LSD varies by ten years, depending on the material it is sold in; a sugar cube is heavier than tissue paper. Recently, Christian Martensen, a twenty-one-year-old who needed money to fix his van, was approached in Tucson by an undercover agent who offered to pay $400 if Martensen could find him some LSD. Martensen agreed, and because 1.5 grams of LSD was impregnated in heavy blotter paper weighing more than 100 grams, he was sentenced to ten years. This was the same sentence given to a supplier found with 20,000 doses on him. As Martensen's lawyer said, "He needed a wake-up call. He didn't need to have his life ruined."

One Pennsylvania judge resigned from the bench after state sentencing guidelines forced her to sentence a young father with no record to five years because, slightly drunk and despondent over the loss of his job, he used a toy gun to rob a taxi driver of fifty dollars. Federal judge J. Lawrence Irving, a Reagan appointee, also recently resigned in protest: "You've got murderers who get out sooner than some kid who did some stupid thing with drugs."

A few years ago OSHA decided that workers needed more protection from hazardous chemicals. The scheme OSHA came up with was to require every maker of a hazardous substance to send an informational sheet with every package or container. These Material Safety Data Sheets

(MSDS) describe the possible harmful effects of each item. Every workplace must keep notebooks of MSDS forms at designated locations around the workplace. The idea seemed perfectly reasonable; there would be a ready reference for assessing the effects of hydrochloric acid and other hazardous chemicals.

But OSHA couldn't restrain itself. The MSDS forms had to apply universally to everything that could conceivably have a toxic effect. The OSHA list of possible toxic substances now totals over 600,000 products, and new items are added constantly. In 1991, OSHA turned its attention again to bricks — not to how bricks are manufactured, but to whether warnings against brick poisoning are needed for people who use them.

Bricks can fall on people, but never have bricks been considered poisonous. In 1991, the OSHA regional office in Chicago, after visiting a construction site, sent a citation to the brick maker for failing to supply an MSDS form with each pallet of bricks. If a brick is sawed, OSHA reasoned, it can release small amounts of the mineral silica. The sawing of bricks, however, does not release large amounts, and bricklayers don't spend much time sawing bricks. Bricks, after all, are not used like lumber.

Brick makers thought the government had gone crazy. According to Bob Hrasok, "You have more exposure driving down a dusty road with the window open than working with bricks." Brick manufacturers dutifully began sending out the MSDS

54

form, which describes, for the benefit of workers, how to identify a brick (a "hard ceramic body . . . with no odor") and giving its boiling point (above 3500° F). The problem, at least as seen by the brick manufacturers, was not just the paperwork, but the necessary implication that the material is, in fact, hazardous. In our litigation-crazy society, these forms were an invitation to lawsuits.

In 1994, after several years of fighting, the brick industry succeeded in reversing OSHA's designation of bricks as poisonous. But thousands of other common substances are still on the list. Two years ago a two-person company in Florida was cited for not having MSDS forms for the Windex and Joy cleaning solutions that were found on the premises. The head of OSHA was put in the awkward position of defending the rules:

> While it may sound odd to require information on some household chemicals, in the workplace these chemicals are often used in higher concentrations . . .

Windex? Another employer was cited for not putting a warning label on table salt. All these things can be bad for you. The law is just trying to treat every potentially harmful substance uniformly. But as Professor Aaron Wildavsky pointed out, you can drown in water.

As far as Ron Smeal can tell, no worker at the Glen-Gery plant has ever looked in an MSDS notebook. While walking around the factory to-gether, we went over to one of the notebooks, dutifully hanging from a massive pillar. It was caked thick with dust.

Compulsive devotion to uniformity in law can generally be achieved only by infidelity to fairness in life. Justice Cardozo understood our inclination toward universal rules, but cautioned that "uni-formity of method will carry us upon the rocks" and that "the curse of this fluidity, of an ever-shifting approximation, is one that the law must bear," or "curses yet more dreadful will be invited in exchange." One of the dreadful curses is that we are making diversity illegal.

Making Diversity Illegal

Precise regulation carries with it the necessity to decide exactly what everything should look like. OSHA officials ponder, as best they can, exactly what every safety feature of a factory should be. State regulators of nursery schools and kindergartens scratch their heads to come up with every detail. Not surprisingly, what they dream up, and then turn into law, is their view of the ideal facility. It is as if the illustrator Norman Rockwell had been made dictator and ordered everyone to do things his way.

Jane O'Reilly runs a small nursery school in suburban Boston that has three teachers for thirty children. Under Massachusetts day care regula-

56

tions, it must be run by a teacher with almost the equivalent of a master's degree and can have no more than ten children per teacher. Such expertise and attention is hard to quibble with. It sounds fantastic. But why did children of prior generations have higher test scores? And why does a country like Japan, which often has thirty children per teacher at this age level, have a superior educational system?

At least the requirements just mentioned have a plausible connection to the quality of care. Other rules seem to exist, well, just to make sure everything has a rule. A complete change of clothing for each child must be kept on hand in case of spilling or soiling. Storage of thirty separate outfits is a problem; Ms. O'Reilly wonders why she can't just keep several sets of generic "emergency" clothes for needed occasions.

Inspectors from the Massachusetts Office of Children come regularly, and they always find violations. Their citations have included a cobweb on the bathroom ceiling and liquid dishwashing soap within reach of children (it is used for bubble blowing). The inspectors recently required Ms. O'Reilly to bolt the wooden toy refrigerator to the wall. The toy refrigerator, needless to say, had never posed a problem, but you never know. The only thing the regulators don't do much of is evaluate the quality of the nursery school, for example, by checking with parents and by observing its operation for extended periods.

The ideal day care center that law mandates

is, by definition, nearly perfect. Measured by law, New York's day care centers are even better than those in Massachusetts. New York requires a separate bathroom for teachers and includes a legal dictate to "comfort a child when in distress." Just think of all the miserable children in Massachusetts, wailing without the benefit of this law. New York requires each day care center to fill out a sixty-eight-page, single-spaced checklist with items such as: "Children are never left alone in the classroom." It is unclear what purpose is to be served by these declarations of innocence — is anyone going to admit to being negligent? — or who reads them.

Regulation like this is not pleasant for the individuals actually trying to care for children. "All I do is scrape people off the floor all day," said one New York day care inspector. They are "terrified about breaking the rules." And why shouldn't they be? When the law loses its connection to common sense, no internal compass can guide people as to right and wrong.

The ideal day care center does not, of course, come cheap. Annual tuition generally costs over $4,000 in Massachusetts. What happens to the parents who cannot afford this Norman Rockwell vision? Again we get the paradox of too much law.

Child care has been driven underground into a world where there are no regulatory protections. Approximately 80 percent of all children are cared for in unregulated facilities, many in illegal day

care operations. Severe overcrowding or dangerous facilities go unnoticed, a fact horribly brought
to light several years ago by a fire in a New
York City home from which children could not
escape the basement where they were illegally
allowed to play.

Less idealized rules would permit affordable day
care for parents who can't possibly pay $4,000
for each child while still providing a basic oversight function. This would require, however, accepting the idea that everything can't be perfect.

Building codes, perhaps the least controversial
of all regulatory laws, cause a similar problem.
They dictate minimum room dimensions, require
that bathrooms and kitchens be separate from
rooms for every other use, and mandate hundreds
of other details. Good ideas and technological advances fill every page of the code book. Who
can object to any of this?

No one, provided society can afford it. One
of the causes of homelessness (probably third in
importance, after mental illness and substance
abuse) is the shortage of low-cost housing. We
made slums illegal and then, with our building
codes, made it impossible to build low-cost
housing.

The virtual extinction of single-room-occu-
pancy buildings illustrates the side effects of this
drive toward mandated perfection. Until the mid-
1980s, most cities had tried to get rid of so-called
SROs, the last remaining cheap housing, until they
realized that the only alternative for most SRO

occupants was the street. Cities abruptly reversed course and passed laws prohibiting the demolition of the SROs. But it was too late. Most were gone. The law now prohibits the demolition of any SROs that remain, while building codes make it impossible to build any new ones.

In 1986, Chris Mortenson, a San Diego developer, realized you could build profitable SROs if you ignored the building code, and commissioned an architect to see what he could come up with. The result was a four-story building with ten-by-twelve-foot units, about half the size required by the building code. Each had a microwave, a sink, and a toilet (partitioned but not separated). Communal showers were at the end of each hall. Rule after rule in the building code was broken. After extensive negotiation, San Diego waived the building code. The building was built for less than $15,000 per unit, and immediately reached 100 percent occupancy. Housing was thereby made available to people who could afford fifty dollars per week but not a hundred.

Real people tend to have their own way of doing things — a little borrowed, a little invented, and so forth. Law, trying to make sure nothing ever goes wrong, doesn't respect the idiosyncrasy of human accomplishment. It sets forth the approved methods, in black and white, and that's that. When law notices people doing it differently, its giant heel reflexively comes down.

Paul Atkinson operates a farm near Eugene,

Oregon, producing hand-raised chemical-free pork and lamb and, until recently, goat cheese. His customers include some of the best restaurants in the country, including, for example, Bouley in lower Manhattan. Cheese-making regulations specify precisely the types of equipment that can be used and require they be stainless steel. By contrast, Europeans, who supply most of our goat cheese, often make it in traditional wood vats. Several years ago an inspector told Mr. Atkinson that his pasteurizing vat, although made of steel, was not of the standard design, and ordered him to get rid of it. It didn't matter that Mr. Atkinson's cheese was found to be clean. The inspector also thought the walls were "too rough" and required Mr. Atkinson to recoat them with plaster and several coats of paint. Shortly thereafter, Mr. Atkinson closed down the cheese facility because "the regulatory requirements make it unprofitable." What annoyed him the most were the "preordained regulations." If the cheese meets the standards, he asked, "why can't the farmer produce the cheese however he wants?"

Gary Cuissey and a partner have run a tiny coffee shop in New York's Little Italy for years. Recently Kent Barwick, former City Landmarks commissioner, stopped in for breakfast and was dismayed to be served with disposable plates and forks. Gary reported that the restaurant inspectors had been by and told him the law would not let him operate if he continued to wash dishes by hand. The code requires an automatic dishwasher, or a chemical process. But chemicals are impractical, and Gary's coffee shop is so small that it has no room for a dishwasher. The only solution was disposables. Now everything is plastic.

Columnist Russell Baker, pondering why all shopping malls seemed to be identical, concluded that it was probably one mall traveling around the country at the speed of light. Modern law is trying to mall-ize every regulated activity. The main victims are small enterprises, poorer segments of society, and the spirit of ingenuity on which this country achieved its greatness.

And why do you think the malls all look alike?

A LAW OF ANGLES

Producing rules at the speed of fast forward may not produce the benefits of certainty, but it creates endless opportunities for slick operators. No one else can understand the garble. To smart lawyers, an entire world of angles and advantage opens up. The classic example is the billionaire who pays no taxes. Wherever there is legal complication, let the games begin.

But why should this be? Precise rules, most people believe, "close off loopholes." It happens to be the other way around. Loopholes only exist because of precise rules. The Constitution, a short document of general principles, has no loopholes. The tax law, all 36,000 pages of it, is practically nothing but loopholes. The more precise we try to make law, the more loopholes are created. If EPA were trying to protect free speech, it would define *speech* in dozens of pages and have hundreds of exceptions. Just as with all the rules discussed above, they would still dictate the wrong results, or require further interpretation, in the next problem that arose. The Constitution, on the other hand, uses ten words: "Congress shall make no law . . . abridging the freedom of speech." It too requires interpretation, but the interpretation relates to the broad purpose, freedom of speech, not to the meaning of the defining words.

Modern law is a game of parsing and logical intrigue. Wherever detailed provisions bend and twist, the observant lawyer will find a place where he can go and violate the spirit of the rules, or get an advantage over others, and do so with complete impunity.

The point of the criminal-sentencing grid was to eliminate unevenness in the sentences meted out by judges. Fairness suffered in the pursuit of uniformity, but as often happens, uniformity has suffered from manipulation of the underlying criteria. Policemen and prosecutors now huddle over the complex 258-box grid in their offices, figuring out how to make arrests so that they can maximize sentences and gain more leverage. Meanwhile, the judges' hands are tied by the sentencing grid. For those who fear abuse of government power, like the reformers who wanted to eliminate judicial discretion, there could be no worse result. Judges, at least, are impartial.

And there was the effort by Congress in 1992 to protect consumers from high cable TV prices, hailed as the "most important consumer victory of the past 20 years." Five hundred pages of detailed rules knocked down high rental charges for converter boxes and remote control units. A formula would ensure that prices were related to actual cost; basic service charges would be based on the number of channels offered. The effect? Nothing, except that prices edged up. Operators more than made up any decline in prices by increasing installation costs (which had previously been done below cost). They manipulated the basic service charges by changing the number of channels a subscriber had to buy. It was hopeless: Trying to detail cable charges just ended up giving operators a chance to blame increases on the government. Congress, looking foolish, is coming up with a new scheme.

Detailing rules can also provide intentional loopholes, giving Congress the chance to appear fair while helping a favored constituency. In 1990, Congress passed an immigration act which provided that, for three years, no less than 40 percent of visas should go to "the foreign state the natives of which received the greatest number of visas" under an earlier law. Which country is it? One hint: Senator Pat Moynihan is a very effective legislator. As Professor Peter Schuck has noted, "Without quite naming the Irish, the statute created a special new preference

64

for them and concealed it."

Litigation is the insiders' game within the game. It is a world in which lawyers manipulate the detailed rules of procedure to harass the other side and delay for years any reckoning for their clients' conduct. As books by Peter Huber and Walter Olson demonstrate, litigation has become shamefully cynical. Judges, acting more like referees, are unwitting accomplices; the rules, after all, permit all these devices. Without the steady application of the judges' view of what is really happening, litigation becomes a tool of manipulation. Staying power — who has the most money — is as important as the merits of the cases.

Law, supposedly the backdrop for society, has been transformed into one of its main enterprises. For billionaires, cable TV companies, law enforcement officers, congressmen, and litigators, close scrutiny and manipulation of the rules is a means to an end. The words of law give them lower taxes, a way to avoid price controls, longer sentences, a secret means of playing favorites, and a tool to grind the other side into the ground.

RESPONDING BY CONVULSIONS

Several years ago, there were horror stories of workers who were asphyxiated and had died in a meat-packing plant while checking on a giant vat of animal blood. Then it happened again at the same plant. OSHA had done virtually nothing, however, because it had no rule that applied to the situation. Stretched thin giving out citations all across America for infractions like improper railing height, OSHA also had not reinspected a plant that had admittedly "deplorable" conditions. Confronted with its own ineptitude, OSHA's response was to pass a universal rule requiring the installation of atmospheric testing devices in all confined spaces, without exception.

But many confined spaces in workplaces don't pose any risk. Glen-Gery, for example, has large bins in which it stores clay. No one can get inside them unless they're empty. Once a year they are cleaned, and there's never been an incident. But the rule applies. So rather than spend thousands of dollars on atmospheric testing devices, Glen-Gery welded the doors shut. Now, once a year, workers have to open the bins with a blowtorch (not the safest activity), go in and clean them, and then weld them shut again. Because of a safety rule that makes no sense in context, opening a hatch with a handle is now a job for a blowtorch.

The savings-and-loan crisis prompted a new law designed to solve the problem of undercapitalized banks once and for all. The new law (portentously called the Financial Institution Reform, Recovery and Enforcement Act, or FIRREA) imposes detailed capital ratios and formulas, no exceptions permitted. Without question, the law ensures that there will be no more sick banks. What we get instead are more dead banks, at much greater expense to taxpayers. The new rules turn any bank needing capital into a pariah to potential investors. The risk of regulatory seizure (the phrase regulators use) is too great under the new law. Government, believing it can only act through specific dictates, lurches again to solve yesterday's problem.

Government's convulsions are most dramatic when it deals with toxic risk, which former EPA head William Reilly has described as regulation "by episodic panic." Sensationalistic press is part of the problem, and Congress, confronted with something bad, perceives the need to promise to eradicate all evil. No cost should be spared, you might suggest, where poisons that could affect human life are concerned. But the costs of these regulations are a real expense, like a tax, and there are countless public purposes in need of funding. Not weighing them against each other is to act like a manic spendthrift, randomly using up resources without any thought of tomorrow. Nor is it a choice of protection or no protection: Often, as one EPA official observed, 95 percent of a toxic problem can be solved quickly and efficiently, but it takes years and billions to solve a problem completely.

But most environmental and safety mandates, laid out in legal black and white, ignore cost and preclude balancing. Some regulations cost over $100 million per statistical life saved, which implies that we would dedicate the entire GNP to prolonging the lives of 1 out of 5,000 citizens. The irony of our emotional approach to toxic control is that it ends up killing people. As Justice Stephen Breyer observed in his book *Breaking the Vicious Cycle,* there is an "income effect" from spending money on nonproductive activities like cleaning dirt. If the money were in the economy, there would be more jobs and less stress. According to economists' studies, every 1 percent increase in unemployment over time is correlated with 19,000 more deaths by heart attack and 1,100 more suicides. That works out to about 4 unnecessary deaths for the $30 million spent on a typical cleanup, and 14 deaths on a $100 million regulation that saves 1 life. The late Aaron Wildavsky, in an article entitled "The Secret of Safety Lies in Danger," described how, time and again, a headlong rush to cure a problem perfectly often leads to more harm.

Everything is interconnected. Just as we make choices whether to drive in a blizzard or buy a house in a district with good schools, every decision involves benefits and risks. Every situation is different. Judgment and balancing are always required. The words of law can't provide the final wisdom.

LOSING RESPECT FOR LAW

Law was always the pride of our country. It was the common framework within which a free people could take their own path to fulfillment. The addition of regulatory law, as Professor Edward Rubin has observed, "did not arise out of some lapse of moral vigilance." We wanted it to protect common resources, like air and water, and to advance other common goals. Most of these regulatory goals enjoy wide support.

Yet, increasingly, law makes us feel like its victims. We divert our energies into defensive measures designed solely to avoid tripping over rules that seem to exist only because someone put them there. Knowing for certain that full compliance is impossible, and that the government's formalistic reaction may be wholly out of proportion, law has fostered what Professor Joel Handler has described as a "culture of resistance."

> Instead of fostering cooperation it destroys it. By emphasizing violations rather than problems, regulation creates bitterness and adversariness. Everything must be put on the record. Businesses will not share information. A culture of resistance sets in.

New rules are looked upon with resignation and are often considered, as one prominent lawyer put it, to be "transient, boring, and hardly worthy of serious study." Indeed, unless getting caught is a real risk, why should we comply with these rules? Are we at the point, as Bayless Manning feared, where "a scofflaw attitude has become accepted" by the public? When law is too dense to be known, too detailed to be sensible, and is always tripping us up, why should we respect it?

Perhaps we should recall President Clinton's search for his attorney general. Rules about withholding taxes on a babysitter's wages, extremely precise, turn out to be widely ignored by some of the most prominent lawyers in the country. President Clinton was able to resolve the crisis, not by finding a law-abiding paragon (although I still can't figure out what Judge Kimba Wood did wrong), but by appointing an attorney general who was childless. The episode was absurd, like a skit on late-night television. It was as if the nation had been locked in a vacuum chamber devoid of proportion or common sense.

Law itself, not the goals to be advanced by law, is now our focus. Indeed, the main lesson of law without judgment is that law's original goal is lost. Safety inspectors wander around without even thinking about safety. The YMCA of New York City, one of the last providers of transient housing at low cost for visitors, gets regular citations for code violations like nonaligning windows and closet doors that do not close tightly. Does the city think that those rooms, by all accounts clean and inexpensive, are somehow unworthy of a city that itself provides cots eighteen inches apart for those who have no place to sleep? A city inspector recently told the YMCA, after it had virtually completed a renovation, that the fire code had changed and a different kind of fire alarm system, costing another $200,000, would have to be installed. "Don't they realize that the $200,000," said Paula Gavin, the president of New York's YMCA, "can provide year-long programs for a hundred kids?"

What are we doing?

REMEMBERING RATIONALISM AND KILLING IT AGAIN

Rationalism, the bright dream of figuring out everything in advance and setting it forth precisely in a centralized regulatory system, has made us blind. Obsessed with certainty, we see almost nothing. We bolt a toy refrigerator to the wall and demand 42-inch-high railings without checking whether the day care center is a nurturing environment or the factory is actually safe.

Friedrich Hayek, the Austrian-American economist and Nobel laureate, devoted much of his brilliant career to describing how rationalism could never work. How can anything good happen, Hayek asked, if individuals cannot think and do for themselves? Rules preclude initiative. Regimentation precludes evolution. Letting accidents happen, mistakes be made, results in new ideas. Trial and error is the key to all progress. The Soviet system of rules and central planning is doomed to failure, Hayek stated with confidence fifty years ago, because it kills the human faculty that makes things work.

We too have deluded ourselves into thinking

that government should only act through central, self-executing rules. Although for different reasons, we too have this egotistical belief that we can make government operate like a Swiss watch, tolerating no exception or uncertainty, and haven't made the connection to the centrally planned system that we so loathed. We have cast aside our good sense, and worship an icon of abstract logic and arbitrary words.

Look up at the Tower of Babel we are erecting in worship of perfectly certain and self-regulating authority. It admits no judgment or discretion: that, indeed, is the mortal sin it exists to eradicate. No one should ever, never ever, be allowed to exercise discretion: In matters of regulation, law itself will provide the answer. Sentence by sentence, it prescribes every eventuality that countless rule writers can imagine. But words, even millions of them, are finite. The range of possible future circumstances is infinite. One slip-up, one unforeseen event, and all those logical words turn into dictates of illogic. Too bad — the mountain of lime can't be used for pollution control; the rule says it's hazardous waste, even though everyone knows it's not hazardous at all.

Aristotle, sometimes accused of being the father of rationalism, was the originator of the phrase "government by laws, not men." But the father of rationalism understood that reason only carries you so far and that implementation must always leave room for us to adjust for the circumstances: "[I]t is impossible that all things should be precisely set down in writing; for enactments must be universal, but actions are concerned with particulars."

When American legal scholars had writhed for decades following Holmes's pronouncement that certainty was dead, Cardozo stepped forward to explain why "over-emphasis on certainty may lead us to . . . intolerable rigidity." "Justice," he noted, "is a concept by far more subtle and indefinite than is yielded by mere obedience to a rule."

Cardozo was sympathetic to the quest for certainty — he said he was "disheartened" when he realized there was no "solid land of fixed and settled rules" — but explained that it was not achievable:

No doubt the ideal system, if it were attainable, would be a code at once so flexible and so minute, as to supply in advance for every conceivable situation the just and fitting rule. But life is too complex to bring the attainment of this idea within the compass of human power.

No "body of information [can] be fed into a computer," Vaclav Havel has noted, in the hope that sooner or later "it will spit out a universal solution."

Law cannot promise a uniformity that is available on paper but never in actual conduct. Different judges do not decide the same cases the same way. The jury system does not produce results like a scientific theorem; it is more akin to a roll of the dice. But a jury is impartial, and it can weigh all the circumstances. That's the best we can do.

We would revolt if government tried to prohibit us from standing on a chair to reach something on a high shelf, or restricted the number of cups of coffee we drink, or told us how to clean our house. But that is the level of detail of modern regulatory law. We suffer it as individuals mainly through institutions like schools, hospitals, and places of work. But these institutions are a large part of our lives, and wrap closely around us. The thin separation only mutes each indignity, causing an overall ache and making it hard to pinpoint the cause. We don't revolt mainly because we don't understand.

Law is not coercive, Hayek noted, if "it permits you to adapt." But if it tells you exactly what to do, it has all the characteristics of coercion. Coercion by government, the main fear of our founding fathers, is now its common attribute. But it was not imposed to advance some group's selfish purpose; we just thought it would work better this way. The idea of a rule detailing everything has had the effect of reversing the role of law. We now have a government of laws against men.

Rationalism looms before us with more logic and reasons than we can possibly respond to, demanding almost all our energy, but ultimately not making any sense. We must kill it again.

This time, however, it will take no cold war or arms race: All we have to do is recognize it for what it is. "The era of absolutist reason is drawing to a close," Havel warned the Western democracies in 1992, and "it is high time to draw conclusions from that fact."

II

THE BUCK
NEVER
STOPS

I n 1962, Rachel Carson shocked the nation, and helped give birth to the environmental movement, by exposing the effects of DDT and other pesticides in her influential book *Silent Spring*. There was also another side to the issue: Pesticides give us apples without worms and the most productive farms in the world. In 1972, Congress required the newly created Environmental Protection Agency to review all pesticides and decide which should be removed from the market. The Federal Insecticide, Fungicide and Rodenticide Act gave EPA three years to make this review, which involved, as it turned out, about six hundred chemical compounds. Over twenty years have now passed. For most of this time, upward of a thousand EPA employees have been working on the pesticide project. Should we feel confident that a perfect head of lettuce is also reasonably safe?

It turns out that EPA has only gotten around to judging the safety of about thirty pesticides. Hundreds of others, including ones on which there are data of significant risk, have continued to be marketed without a decision. "At this rate," said Jim Aidala, an expert on pesticides who worked for Congress, "the review of existing pesticides will be completed in the year 15000 A.D."

The two-decade delay on the review of pesticides is not unusual. In 1962 the Food and Drug Administration was ordered to review the two hundred or so existing food-color additives for harmful effects. The timetable was thirty months. The project was finally completed in 1990, twenty-eight years later.

The Abyssinian Baptist Church in Harlem struggled for four years to get approval for a Head Start program in a newly renovated building. Most of the time was spent arguing with bureaucrats about the dimensions of rooms that did not satisfy standard guidelines. "An entire generation of Head Starters missed the facility," said Karen Phillips from the church. "The people in Washington want to tell you this or that can't be done. I told them, 'I know you're talking about five pieces of paper, but we're talking about children.' They didn't seem too interested in common sense."

Making decisions, it almost seems too obvious to say, is necessary to do anything. Staying with the obvious, every decision involves a choice; otherwise there would be no need to decide. And almost every choice has a negative effect: The Head Start program gets approved with nonstandard rooms or there is no program there; EPA bans the pesticide or not with direct impact on its maker or on consumers. Not choosing is not benign: We may eat something bad because the

EPA never got around to making a decision.

"The problem with government," Brookings economist Charles Schultze told me one day, "is that it can't ever be seen to do any harm." Even helping can be a form of harm; it might be viewed as favoritism. So, Schultze noted, very few decisions get made. The lag in decision making, one observer noted, is a national scandal.

Novocaine seems to have been injected into bureaucrats' brains, at least into the lobe where the word *yes* is found. Reasons flow out why nothing can happen, but getting anyone to say yes is like scaling a mountain. "It's just so frustrating," said Rev. Calvin Butts of the Abyssinian Church, "that many people don't even bother to try anymore."

It's not that bureaucrats don't like us. They do it to themselves as well, and the disease, or whatever it is, has advanced rapidly in recent decades. Sam Schwartz, a government engineer who was deputy commissioner of New York's Transportation Agency, was hired in 1974. The hiring process took two days: He had an interview on Thursday and was asked to start the following Monday. Hiring in the same agency twenty years later, Mr. Schwartz notes, takes up to five months. The process, designed for openness to make sure the best candidates are looked at, instead means that the best candidates have found work elsewhere and are no longer available. The overall effect of this and other blockages in making decisions in the agency, according to another former deputy, is a pervasive "culture of defeatism."

81

Sometimes government cannot act even in the face of imminent peril. In the early morning hours of April 13, 1992, in the heart of Chicago's downtown Loop, the Chicago River broke through the masonry of an old railroad tunnel built in the last century. Several hundred million gallons of water from the river were diverted from Lake Michigan into the basements of downtown office buildings, knocking out boilers, short-circuiting countless electric switches, ruining computers, and turning files into wet pulp. Total losses were over $1 billion. Several weeks before the accident, the leak in the tunnel had come to the attention of John LaPlante, Chicago's transportation commissioner, a public servant with thirty years of exemplary service. He knew that the river was immediately overhead and that a break could be disastrous. He ordered his engineers to shore it up. As a prudent administrator, he also asked how much it would cost. The initial guess was about $10,000. His subordinates then went to a reputable contractor, who quoted $75,000. Although the amount was a drop in the bucket in his huge budget, the discrepancy, seven times the original estimate, gave Commissioner LaPlante pause. He knew exactly what to do. He put it out for competitive bids. Two weeks later, before the process had even begun, the ceiling collapsed.

Bureaucrats in all these stories don't even seem to be looking in the right direction. What we would consider the goals — fixing the leak right away, opening another Head Start program in

Harlem, taking a bird in the hand when a good young engineer applies for a job — apparently are not important. Something else is: How things are done has become far more important than what is done.

The utopian urge that prompted us in recent decades to write the world's thickest instruction manual, naming it the law of the land, has led us to invent a device that, like detailed rules, also avoids the untidiness of human judgment. It goes by an ancient name, process, but its purpose is new. It once existed to help humans make responsible decisions. Process now has become an end in itself.

Just as certainty was the promise held out by detailed rules, process presented itself wearing the velvet cloak of responsibility. And just as rules have turned law against us, the exaltation of process has transformed the idea of fair consideration into ritual without consideration. It has become the orthodoxy of government.

The ceremonies and excuses by which decisions are avoided may surprise you, but the effect will not. Government accomplishes virtually nothing of what it sets out to do. It can barely fire an employee who doesn't show up for work.

Not deciding is not a new phenomenon. Every bureaucrat worth his salt, from the pharaoh's court in ancient Egypt to the blame-layers in the final days of the Bush administration, learns how to protect his position by passing the buck. The difference today is that we have decided to exalt what used to be considered an unfortunate weakness of human nature. Not taking responsibility is now institutionalized in layers of forms and meetings.

Soon after the Civil Service Act in 1883, at the beginning of America's modern bureaucracy, Woodrow Wilson, a noted political scientist before he became president, emphasized the need to vest public servants with "large powers and . . . discretion" as the indispensable "condition of responsibility." Otherwise, he warned, nothing will get done: "The less his power the more safely obscure and unnoticed does he feel his position to be, the more readily does he relapse into remissness." It is only a slight exaggeration to suggest, as Woodrow Wilson warned, that our entire government has "relapsed into remissness."

Viewed under history's light, it is clear what happened. We have deluded ourselves into thinking that the right decisions will be ensured if we build enough procedural protection. We have accomplished exactly the opposite: Decisions, if they happen at all, happen by default. Public decisions are not responsible because no one takes responsibility.

Commissioner LaPlante in fact had the authority to spend $75,000 to fix the leak; every procedure has an exception for emergencies. But he apparently did not want to take responsibility for that decision. The procedures are there, after all, to make sure he is not careless with the taxpayers' money and does not play favorites with friendly contractors. In a system designed to discourage individual initiative, LaPlante went by the book. And the ceiling fell in.

THE VELVET TRAP OF PROCESS

Process has a comforting sound. By requiring set patterns, it tries to make sure things are done properly. Procedures are installed to prevent cheating or playing favorites. The idea of process is deeply embedded in our culture. Democracy is a process: We vote in elections to pick representatives we hope will make decisions for the common good. "Due process" must be observed before government, under our Constitution, can take away our liberty or property. Most people, if they thought about it, would be in favor of proper procedures. Businesses use procedures to help organize themselves. Families establish procedures for who washes the dishes and takes out the garbage.

But there is a difference between the patterns we set for ourselves and legal process. We use procedures as a management device, always subject to change or exception where a procedure gets in the way of a sensible result. For us, the result is paramount. Legal process comes out of a very different tradition: It is the hallowed protection against government coercion of a citizen. Even a thief caught red-handed is entitled to the presumption of innocence; process is our way of making sure government doesn't barge into our homes and frame us. Constitutional due process is notoriously inefficient. That, indeed, is its purpose. To Daniel Webster, the idea was wrapped up in the thought that the law "hears before it condemns." When Justice Felix Frankfurter declared that "the history of American freedom is . . . the history of procedure," he was absolutely correct: By imposing conditions on coercion, due process ensures our individual freedom.

Fixing a leak in a tunnel, on the other hand, has nothing to do with individual freedom. Banning a pesticide that might poison us certainly affects the manufacturer, but the pesticide manufacturer is not exactly an unsuspecting homeowner who wakes up to find a government bulldozer at his front door. The manufacturer is trying to sell a poison that affects everyone else. Government is our surrogate for deciding whether or not the pesticide should be allowed to be "bought" by us.

But modern process barely distinguishes among the vast range of government acts, and has thrown its cloak over every decision. Ordinary decisions are subject to rigid formalities taken as seriously as the due process protection in a criminal trial. The actual goals of government are treated like a distant vision, displaced by an almost religious preoccupation with procedural conformity.

In the late 1980s, Dr. Michael McGuire, a senior research scientist at UCLA, found himself in trouble. His lab, which sits on five acres, is funded by the Veterans Administration. Its lawn also needs to be cut. When the lawnmower broke, Dr. McGuire decided to go out and buy another one. He filled out no forms and got no approvals. He also told VA mechanics they could use the broken lawnmower for spare parts. During a routine audit, the federal auditor asked why the lawnmower was different. Dr. McGuire told the truth, and thus launched an investigation that resulted in several meetings with high-level federal officials: "I couldn't understand," Dr. McGuire notes, "why important agency officials would spend their time this way." Finally, after months, they rendered their findings: They could find no malice, but they determined Dr. McGuire to be ignorant of the proper procedures. He received an official reprimand and was admonished to study VA procedures ("about the size of an encyclopedia"). Dr. McGuire has not yet achieved the proper state of contrition: "I guess I made the egregious mistake of tossing a broken federal lawnmower." One other fact: Dr. McGuire bought the lab's lawnmower with his own money.

Individual initiative in government has shriveled up and lies dormant. Process has, indeed, rendered initiative unlawful. The Carroll Street Bridge in Brooklyn, built in 1889, was the nation's first retractable bridge; it slid back and forth across the Gowanus Canal on heavy rails, like a slide rule. By the mid 1980s, it was in disrepair; it could no longer carry traffic and was a barrier between neighborhoods. In 1988 the city budgeted

$3.5 million for an overhaul. Under procurement procedures, it was estimated that bidding would take two years, and the work at least five years. But with the bridge's 100th anniversary coming up, Sam Schwartz, the deputy commissioner responsible for bridges, had the idea that the Carroll Street Bridge should be fixed within the year, in time for a centennial party. Schwartz called in his chief engineer and asked him to draw up a repair plan, ignoring the contracting procedures. He also told him to try to fix up all its architectural decoration, not part of the approved work plan. Without much trouble, notwithstanding all the oversight agencies supposedly checking up to make sure everything is done by the book, Schwartz got the money and let the contracts.

Eleven months later, at a cost of $2.5 million, the bridge was fixed up. Practically the entire neighborhood participated in the centennial party, by all accounts a wonderful affair. For his leadership in completing the job in one seventh of the time and at 70 percent of budget, Deputy Commissioner Schwartz received an official reprimand.

The procedures Schwartz ignored — over thirty-five steps, involving six agencies and generally taking at least two years before any work can begin — exist to ensure complete neutrality and to protect against fraud. The fact that Schwartz was willing to stand up and take responsibility (and saved the city an estimated $1 million) was irrelevant. The ritual had been violated.

Irregularities are dangerous, someone might argue; these procedures serve important practical purposes, like preventing fraud and getting the best price, and it would be unwise to permit exceptions. But serving practicality, as anyone within ten miles of a government contract knows, is the last thing these procedures do. Their inefficiency, for reasons we will visit, is legendary. Fraud, notwithstanding all the procedural layers, happens all the time. Deputy Commissioner Schwartz certainly had no trouble getting around all the oversight procedures.

Orthodoxy, not practicality, is the foundation of process. Its demons are corruption and favoritism, but the creed of this orthodoxy is a perfect uniformity. Only if all things are done the same way can government be fair. Sameness, everywhere for everybody, is the operating instruction of modern government. It was not fair for Mr. Schwartz just to go out and negotiate a contract with whomever he and his engineers trusted. What about all the other contractors in the area not even given a chance at the work? As Edward Fygi, the general counsel of the United States Department of Energy put it, "It's about the same standard as a court. Government must act as an impartial decision maker, giving everyone equal access and a fair shot at the contract."

Well, why not? Government should lean over backward, many will suggest, to make sure everything it does can satisfy a broader goal of equal treatment of all its citizens. It is, after all, *government* that we're talking about. But concepts like equality and consistency are absolute; they have no logical stopping point; there is no place where they say, "Oh, I certainly didn't mean that a broken lawnmower should be treated as a federal case," or "The Chicago commissioner shouldn't worry about bidding procedures with the river only a few feet above the leak." Where do you draw the line? No one wants to take that risk, so the line is never drawn. Shuffling to the rhythms of process, answering any potential complaint with one more procedure, becomes what government does.

What this means in practice may surprise you.

LIKE MICE ON A WHEEL

Consider the discovery of a sagging floor. If you owned the building, you would probably call an engineer you knew and ask him to make a report. If you were very cautious, you might interview a few engineers of good reputation, have a discussion about the problem and their rates, and then make a decision. The entire process might take two hours, or a day or two at most.

Satisfying universal fairness is a little tougher. Here's how New York City does it. Lean back: It may take upward of two years. The process starts with "scoping meetings," with bureaucrats from the affected agency and the General Services Agency discussing the problem and the precise work required. Most contracts must be competitively bid, and to make sure every bidder is treated exactly the same, someone is assigned to prepare a detailed work plan that, like a modern rule, tries to foresee every eventuality. Does the engineer need to look under the floorboards, or can he do the work by taking out ceiling tiles on the floor below? It takes a lot of work to do all the work in your head in advance and then to write it all down, but how else can all bids be exactly comparable? Coming up with this description takes several months, and it is then checked by the interested agencies. Finally, a full bidding document, called a "Request for Proposals," is prepared. This package, generally about two inches thick for a small project, also goes through a round of reviews.

Then, you might think, it gets sent out to reputable engineers who have done good work for the city in the past. Unthinkable. That would be considered favoritism. A random drawing is made from a pool of all engineers who have registered for city work; generally, eight are chosen (including several from separate lists of women and minority engineers), and the package is sent out to the lucky winners.

Does the city then sit down and negotiate with engineers who are interested? No, personal factors (or worse) might intrude in personal interviews. The city will consider only comprehensive written submissions. An engineer so desperate for work that he bothers to spend two days on the extensive paperwork (including certifying his equal opportunity employment practices and his refusal to deal with suspect foreign countries) sends it in, and . . . does someone finally decide? No. Actually, we're just getting going.

Three to five bureaucrats from different agencies are appointed as a committee to review the submissions. Then they decide? No. They can't just decide; somebody on the committee might skew the deliberations by force of personality or, who knows, might be on the take. A point system is utilized in which each member individually and without discussion with others rates the submissions. They then compare point totals. Do they call around to check on reputation? Of course not. Everyone must be treated equally, without the taint of someone's *subjective* evaluation. Only the written submissions are considered, at least at this level.

At this level? Well, you never know, maybe the whole committee was paid off. Careful review of the calculations is made by another, higher-level, committee. Yet another review is made by the Mayor's Office of Contracts.

Then that's it? No. Now we can begin where most people do. We can have a negotiation with the engineer, if he still remembers what it was about. Then there are a few more steps, such as approval by the city comptroller and another approval from the mayor's office. Contracts for big jobs are more extensive, of course; I have seen a chart showing 209 steps for certain capital items. A report of a few years ago, characterizing the city process as "awash in a sea of paper and plagued by inordinate delays," errs on the side of understatement.

And so the sagging floor is eventually looked at. Unless, of course, one of the unsuccessful bidders complains that a mistake was made or the process was unfair. Then the contract is put on hold while lawyers try to resolve the matter. "Complete objectivity is the goal," one deputy commissioner told me. "Otherwise," he was instructed when he started the job, "unfair factors might be considered."

A CASTE OF THE MISTRUSTED

Remember how hard it is for words to specify the characteristics of a safe hammer? A few years ago the federal government bought hammers with a specification that was thirty-three pages long; pity the bureaucrat's spouse at dinner during all the months of drafting. ("Have you ever noticed how hammers are heavier at one end?") Why not just trust the person to go out and buy hammers?

Requiring bureaucrats to engage in these useless exercises turns them into the creatures Americans love to loathe. Harvard professor Steven Kelman, who has been brought to Washington to help Al

Gore address contracting inefficiencies, told of a bureaucrat who bragged that he was "objective enough" not to share information with the federal government's version of the point-calculating committee. The unfairly prejudicial information? The vendor had always performed terribly. According to Kelman:

> Our system for managing the public sector may rob the people in it of their faculties to such an extent that, like a person on a mind numbing drug, they no longer even realize that they are missing anything.

Many bureaucrats see it happening to them, but that's the career they've chosen. What can they do? One experienced bureaucrat put it this way: "What you are is just a person of record. You know, there are days when the biggest decision I made was who gets the desk near the window." A more common response, according to an observer, is "to live a make-believe life of hustle and bustle, taking on the affectations that help sustain the illusion of power." When John Rollwagon, the head of Cray Research who was agonizing through the confirmation procedures to be President Clinton's deputy secretary of commerce, decided to withdraw, he described his experience as follows:

> The only analogy I can make is that I'm an air-breathing animal and I somehow

jumped in the deep end of the pool and I
— I'm not able to grow gills fast enough.
It's such a different environment — working
in the government. Until you're literally inside, you don't quite know what it is.

Mr. Rollwagon was in the impossible position
of being near someone else's taint; his company's
stock had been traded unlawfully. It didn't matter
that he was blameless.

The fixation on corruption is as powerful as
the aversion to human judgment. Every official
act, the procedures presume, is an irresistible opportunity for crime. Only perpetual ritual can
suppress the original sin of corruption that all
bureaucrats acquire when they take their jobs.
Over and over, the ritual tells bureaucrats they
aren't trustworthy. Every breath could be an unlawful tip; better have another procedure. The
New York Metropolitan Transit Authority has
procedures that forbid bus drivers from unjam-
ming coins stuck in the slot on the coin box.
Who knows the temptation of that quarter, its
edge pointing longingly in the driver's direction.

A United States ambassador recounted why he
rarely entertained dignitaries in the official residence and instead used local restaurants that cost
"two or three times as much." Eating at home
was a procedural nightmare, because no reimbursement was allowed unless there was a receipt
for each and every ingredient of the meal prepared
at home — every tomato and every after-dinner

mint. With a restaurant, he just sends in his American Express statement. The dark fear that the cook (or the ambassador?) might cheat a little ends up distorting diplomacy and hangs over the preparation for every event. Who knows, maybe the ambassador and the cook are also spies. Make them fill out another form.

All the procedures — taking two years instead of two hours to hire an engineer — produce an abundance of one thing: paper. The circulating of forms and scratching of initials is sort of like a rosary. ("I checked the forms; Who can blame me?; I checked . . ."). Dr. McGuire (of the lawnmower scandal) once ran a psychiatric department at a Veterans Administration hospital, where he was required to verify when everyone came to work by initialing their time cards. Dr. McGuire refused. "How could I confirm that somebody I don't even know showed up for work on time? I didn't even work in the same building with many of them." Dr. McGuire, perhaps born with an attitude problem, earned another official reprimand.

When Joyce Mendelsohn, a public school teacher in New York until 1992, was asked the most difficult part of her job, she unhesitatingly responded: paperwork. "There is endless duplication; I felt like a character out of Dickens." One of the forms is a detailed lesson plan in which teachers must lay out in advance what they're going to teach that day. Ms. Mendelsohn believes it is clearly counterproductive — "You have to remain flexible and creative in what you teach" — but she also knows nobody looks at it. She knows because she frequently filled in the boxes with words like *Mickey Mouse.*

What matters in this bureaucratic world is not that things are approached sensibly but that everything lives up to the precepts of universal fairness and objectivity. People poke fun at the edges, but the ideology is dead serious.

In August 1993, New York City's budget director, Philip Michael, was forced to resign after front-page headlines reported that he had been accused by the city's investigative agency of favoritism to a vendor. Until then, his reputation had been spotless. Formerly the top lawyer in New York's police department and also the city's finance commissioner, he had been called back into public service from the private sector by three different mayors. The episode involved a subsidiary of Lockheed Corporation, which, trying to recover from a parking-violations collection scandal seven years before, had cleaned house and was now doing this work for Boston, Los Angeles, and Washington, among other cities. Lockheed had offered to guarantee New York City $100 million in additional parking-ticket revenues if it would privatize collections. Budget Director Michael and First Deputy Mayor Norman Steisel thought it was a good idea; the city could use an extra $100 million. The commissioner in charge of parking-ticket collections did not agree.

Mr. Michael, according to the investigative report, "openly argued" for the proposal at large meetings and took "affirmative action" by trying to make a deal with the recalcitrant commissioner to get him to test the plan in a pilot project. The other purported evidence of misconduct came from testimony by one bureaucrat that he "almost wet his pants" when he came to a meeting and saw that Mr. Michael, all by himself, had already started talking to a Lockheed representative.

The report cleared Mr. Michael of venal or self-interested behavior. Nothing was hidden. He just thought the proposal was a good idea. But in the sterilized world where everything must be completely neutral, even having a point of view is suspect. "Openly arguing" for it is considered "unethical." "Favoritism" turns out to be a pejorative synonym for enthusiasm. After reading the report, Mayor Dinkins held a press conference at which he admitted it "looked very bad." Philip Michael was forced to resign. Perhaps in part because of this scandal — essentially, a policy disagreement about parking-ticket collection between two of his commissioners — David Dinkins was not reelected mayor of New York City. Philip Michael is doing fine in the real world, as an executive with a large Connecticut company. And we wonder why government fails to attract good people.

"Objectivity," at least in the broader world, only implies decisions based on facts. Objectivity does not preclude judgment or intuition that flows from facts. Judges are supposed to be more objective than anyone, but Justice Cardozo saw their role as balancing "the precepts of jurisprudence and those of reason and good conscience."

Under the definition of objectivity prevailing in government, only a robot is truly adequate to the job. Decisions are supposed to come out of the process after dozens or hundreds of binary calculations. Trying to exercise leadership, as Philip Michael did, is heresy. The lobotomizing effect on bureaucrats only confirms its success: Everything is pure; no one can be blamed.

THE COSTS OF MISTRUST

How well does this system function for us, for the common good? Let's take procurement, in which the main goal, to buy goods and services, is straightforward and relatively easy to evaluate. The waste of public funds caused by the process is almost inconceivable.

Procedural rituals, designed in the name of fairness to potential vendors, are too exasperating for most people, even corporations whose only interest is as seekers of money. Denise Norberg, a small contractor appearing before Congress in 1989 on behalf of the American Subcontractors Association, said government work is avoided because of the "paperwork burdens" and the "confusing, and often contradictory, array of regulations . . . that have no relationship to construction" or, she noted, "even to common sense."

Only 1 of 535 companies invited to bid in New York on a $9 million contract for car services even bothered.

Higher prices, often significantly higher, are the norm. Ms. Norberg testified that the members who do endure the process "routinely bid government work 10 to 30 percent higher than similar work in the private sector," because there is "at least eight times more paperwork than on a similar private job." This is moderate. The cost of elevator work done for New York City is "three to four times the cost in the private sector."

Paying the bureaucrats who prepare the forms and attend the meetings is also costly. One report calculated that a simple purchase of twelve off-the-shelf personal computers at a contract price of $75,000 had an internal processing cost of $65,000. Fixing a $50 lock in a New York public school takes ten steps over a six-month period, including review by someone called the "supervising supervisor." "Otherwise," reporter Terry Golway observed, the "bureaucracy could not function at peak inefficiency." The federal government has estimated that, annually, 289 million hours are spent complying with its procurement procedures.

The rigidity of the procedures, which eliminates the normal give-and-take essential to commercial relationships, means that government regularly buys the wrong thing (or not the right thing). Harvard's Kennedy School of Government has case studies describing this inefficiency in painful detail; in one, North Face, a maker of cold-weather clothing and equipment, tried to comply with government specifications for cold-weather suits. The pieces of fabric (detailed precisely) did not match each other. The zipper was too long (should it dangle down or be sewn around to the other side?). After all these problems were ironed out, the thread (specified over North Face's reservations) cracked when sewn and the suits fell apart. The unfortunate analogy of the Siberian wheat harvest keeps coming to mind.

The amounts at stake are impressive. New York City lets almost 9,000 contracts per year, for $6 billion. For the federal government, the total is $200 billion. For all government entities, the total is $450 billion, or about one tenth our gross national product. The waste is probably not possible to calculate precisely. Is it 20 percent? 30 percent? More? Whatever the amount, it can be fairly described as a chunk out of the budget of every American family. And this is only for the waste attributable to procedures of procurement.

What again, perhaps we should ask, is the purpose of modern process? Staffing procedural fortresses to guard against potential evils is more important than getting anything done: Every tomato the ambassador serves must be accounted for; every stuck quarter in the bus must become unstuck by . . . well, it's unclear, maybe a pothole will jar it loose. Honoring the unknown vendor is more important than getting the best deal. Everything is perfect, at least on paper.

Forms no one reads collect in millions of file cabinets. Mayor Richard Daley of Chicago recently complained that his staff spends four thousand hours a year — the equivalent of two full-time jobs — just signing his name to forms. Is that personal accountability? Never mind. Everything is documented and visible to a mythical central power.

Rationalism rears its head again. Process is a kind of rule. It tells us not what to do, but how to do it. Consistent methods can be useful, depending, of course, on how detailed and unbending the procedure is. Consistency, however, cannot explain the Rube Goldberg procedures required to look at a sagging floor, or the decades-long lag in reviewing pesticides. What explains it is the idea, as described by Max Weber, that the rationalist bureaucracy must always satisfy "formal equality of treatment."

Justifying the fairness of the process has become more important than the goal. Did everything get considered? Could anyone ever criticize our procedures? Government intensely watches itself in the mirror instead of focusing on how to get the job done. Any hair out of place gets the attention of a high-level committee, which fails to notice that the house is falling down.

Even Weber could not have anticipated the extreme to which we have taken "formal equality of treatment." The hallowed techniques of our constitutional system — judicial neutrality and safeguards, legislative committees and votes —

are applied to mundane daily decisions. Every act by government becomes a microcosm of constitutional checks and balances. It is hard to imagine a more exhaustive system unless, I suppose, we had a public referendum on who gets hired and judicial oversight on each contract. (Actually, over 50 percent of federal computer contracts are appealed on the ground of procedural irregularity.)

How government manages itself, which is mainly what we have been discussing, involves no regulation or coercion of citizens. This is where process should be the most utilitarian, a tool for sound management. Instead, it is like a compulsive fetish from which bureaucrats never allow themselves to be diverted. How did we get here?

FROM RITUAL TO RESPONSIBILITY . . .

This was not the original idea of the regulatory state. When the spoils system was replaced by civil service in the 1880s, the goal was eminently practical: Hire qualified people and let them do their best under general rules "without attempting to fill up the minute details." It was explained by one of the sponsors of the Civil Service Reform Act of 1883, Senator Hawley of Connecticut:

> Do not let us indulge an idea that we can make a perfect system and eliminate all evils or possibilities of evil. We can lay out some

general lines . . . [and] say generally . . .
"we hold you . . . responsible for the thor-
ough administration of all affairs . . . under
these general rules."

According to Progressive ideology, the essential
condition of good administration was "freed[om]
from interference by departments organized on
the basis of process." Giving professional civil
servants "large discretion as to the management
of the fires and ovens," wrote Woodrow Wilson
soon after the creation of civil service, would liberate government from the procedural quagmire
of the courts. No procedural protection from the
bureaucrats was needed; neutral professionals
were themselves the protection from unabashed
partisan politics under the spoils system.

Of course, the new bureaucracy never worked
as advertised. The age-old tendency of institutions
to build up layers of process, like sediment on
a harbor bottom, soon also bogged down the bud-
ding regulatory state. Chief Justice Charles Evans
Hughes complained in the 1920s, for example,
about the "mess of administrative pottage, no better for being prepared for democratic cooks." The
temptation to compromise by promising one more
layer of review and oversight is apparently irresistible. But the vision of a neutral expert, liberated from procedure, remained the bureaucratic
ideal.

The New Deal put this ideal to its true test.
With a national crisis and the nation's best talent

flooding into Washington to tackle it, the Roosevelt administration told its recruits to go make decisions. According to a 1937 report to President Roosevelt, process was not important. "Purpose [must be] the central driving force of bureaucracy: . . . Power must be concentrated to be effective and it must be wielded by experts in order to achieve rational results." Jim Landis, Joe Kennedy's successor as chairman of the SEC and one of the young stars of the New Deal, described the philosophy as follows: "One can ask little more than to have issues decided by those best equipped for the task."

Having been given the responsibility to make decisions, the New Deal bureaucrats used it. By today's standards, projects began almost overnight. The Works Progress Administration, among its many projects, constructed hundreds of sewage plants (thereby preserving the purity of the nation's aquifers). In total, it employed 3.5 million people. In less than a year, one program eradicated 7 million disease-carrying rats in six southern states. The Tennessee Valley Authority brought affordable electricity to large parts of the rural South. The courthouses and post offices that we now count among our civic treasures were built during the New Deal.

Individuals were important because they had authority. Perhaps the greatest testimony to their accomplishments is that we still remember their names: Ickes, Tugwell, Hopkins, Landis, Corcoran, Cohen, Douglas, Berle, to name a few. By way of comparison, try naming cabinet members of recent administrations.

The New Deal also had more than a few detractors. Soon after Roosevelt took office, it became apparent that his experts, far from using expertise to achieve ostensibly neutral results, had charted a course that reflected their own political and social views. A drive began to combat what was described as "administrative absolutism." Opponents wanted checks and balances, and at least an opportunity to debate policy before it was implemented.

The idea of fair debate on issues of public importance was, in the end, hard to oppose. Why should bureaucrats be allowed to make decisions without some debate? Government began to circle back toward procedures. Immediately after World War II, the Administrative Procedure Act (known as the APA) was passed as "a bill of rights for all who deal with government."

The procedures imposed by the APA were in fact modest, requiring only public notice and an opportunity for the public to comment before any decisions or rules of general application were made. Politics, not process, was how agencies would be held accountable for these quasi-legislative actions: Go complain to your congressman. Under the APA, no court could overturn one of these decisions unless it was "arbitrary or capricious," the legal equivalent of being in left field. No procedural requirements at all were put on "mere managerial tasks" and other day-to-day activities. Overall, except when an agency acts like a court, agencies retained most of their New Deal power.

Within one generation following the APA, the New Deal blueprint of administrative discretion was dead and forgotten. Remembered as the symbol of big government, the New Deal's condition of effective action — vesting discretion in officials — had been abandoned.

. . . AND BACK TO RITUAL

In 1960, while preparing a special report for President-elect Kennedy, former New Dealer Jim Landis was dismayed to find that the New Deal agencies had become so encrusted with self-imposed rules and procedures that nothing was getting done: "The pressing problem today . . . is to get the administration to assume the responsibilities that it properly should assume." Landis knew the attraction of process to those within government, and called out for leaders who would be willing to take responsibility for administrative decisions:

> Political and official life to too great an extent tends to favor routinization. The assumption of responsibility by an agency is always a gamble that may well make more enemies than friends. The easiest course is frequently that of inaction.

At about the same time that Landis was compiling his report, a new movement called the legal process school was advocating the glorification of process. Government should be remade, this group thought, into a procedural system in which "so far as possible, the individual and the state are placed on a plane of equality." The abuses of McCarthyism and civil rights violations in the South had led them to a heightened distrust of government officials. This distrust developed overpowering momentum during the counterculture revolution during the 1960s.

Their ideal government was modeled on courts. Columbia law professor Harry Jones said in 1958 that dealings with the state should be "as fair, as just and as free from arbitrariness as are the familiar encounters" with the judiciary. Government was too overbearing, argued Yale professor Charles Reich, and should not be allowed to take any action, even the awarding of a contract, without affording the protection of due process. Government should no longer act as it thought best in the common interest; it should be neutral, almost judicial. The rhetoric proved irresistible: Power to the people.

The main legal vehicle, to use the rallying cry of Lyndon Johnson's War on Poverty, was "maximum feasible participation." As one observer noted, "Participation in decision-making, one of the principal ways of achieving due process, is an end in itself. It contributes to rationality, and rationality contributes to effectiveness." New

York City amended its zoning process to have three levels of hearings; environmental review procedures were invented.

Courts led the crusade for more process; after all, the idea was modeled on court procedures. Chief Judge David Bazelon and several colleagues on the federal appeals court in Washington began reversing agency decisions that did not give citizens maximum opportunity to make their point: If a comment was received, the agency had to respond to it fully; if an issue was complicated, the agency had to hold hearings and allow cross-examination. Agencies had to prove they had taken a "hard look" at all the issues. Although cast as a procedural requirement, this "hard look" provision meant that courts could always find a way to overturn any decision they didn't like.

In 1971, the Supreme Court reversed a decision to permit construction of an interstate highway through a portion of Overton Park in Memphis. According to the Court decision, the administrative record was too scanty; more alternatives should have been studied. However unwise the plan to cut through Overton Park, building the highway there in fact had been studied and debated for about twenty years. To government agencies, the lesson was clear: They had to create huge records to justify their decisions.

The right answer would eventually emerge, according to the new approach to government, if only the process were extensive and the bureaucrats took care to be completely objective. As one of the decisions put it, rigorous procedures would "releas[e] the clutch of unconscious preference and irrelevant prejudice." By way of contrast, consider Justice Cardozo's view of the factors that a judge (who holds a more neutral position than a bureaucrat) should use when making a decision: "[I]t will be shaped by his experience in life, his understanding of prevailing canons of justice and morality, his study of social science, and at times, in the end, by his intuition, his guesses . . ."

The simple "notice and comment" requirement of the Administrative Procedure Act had become, by judicial fiat, a celebration of extensive process. Courts, supposedly not in the business of reviewing agency judgments unless they were "arbitrary and capricious," had awarded themselves enormous power.

Substance, of course, underlay all these judgments — the Supreme Court was obviously offended by the decision to put a highway through Overton Park — but no judge would admit simply to disagreeing. If something bad had happened, the procedures must have been improper.

Achieving the requisite state of objectivity became the new bureaucratic preoccupation. In 1978, the breakfast-cereal industry persuaded a court to disqualify the chairman of the Federal Trade Commission, Michael Pertschuk, from participating in a hearing over children's advertising on the basis that he was biased. He had, indeed, given speeches decrying the manipulative ads on

110

children's television. The Federal Trade Commission, however, is a regulatory agency, not a court. Is it the job of the chairman to lead the agency with a point of view or to preside over a trial in which evidence is formally presented? On appeal, the disqualification was reversed; the reasoning, however, was not that Pertschuk should have a point of view, but rather that the industry had not proved he had finally made up his mind on the issues.

Life in government, naturally risk-averse in the best of circumstances, was now defined by procedural fairness. When in doubt, have another round of process. Anyone upset? Have a hearing. Still upset? Have another hearing. *Still* upset? We'll order a new study or organize a task force. Any phone call, any ill-timed remark, pulled out of proceedings that lasted years, could be blown up into a claim of prejudice. A rule of the Department of Education prohibited participation in certain decisions by any bureaucrats who had a "professional interest." Woodrow Wilson and Jim Landis would be agape: The original point of bureaucracy was to have professional points of view.

No one worried much about how government actually got things done. Nor did anyone analyze whether anything important came out of all the mandatory hearings or whether the minute detail of environmental impact statements, hundreds of pages long, illuminated or obscured environmental problems. The procedures, everyone thought, would simply make decisions fairer. To these innovators of procedure, government was government. It would never be efficient, but now it would be completely fair, even pure.

Just as lawyers in the last century were raised by Blackstone's treatise to believe that judges somehow "discovered" true law, recent generations of law students have been raised to believe that multiple procedures represent the true model of how government should be run. According to one recent proposal, the right to counsel in certain kinds of hearings should include a right to additional counsel to review the first counsel's work.

And so it happened that in slightly less than a century, we traveled full circle. The founders of modern bureaucracy sought to make government effective by liberating it from the tangled world of procedural delay and lawyers' tricks. We have now circled back to the world where people argue, not about right and wrong, but about whether something was done the right way. Bureaucracy, founded to liberate government from process, does almost nothing else.

STARING INTO THE LIGHTS, WAITING TO SEE TRUTH

Out of a volcanic cauldron of information and public participation emerges, like the first strands of DNA, the right regulatory answer.

This almost primeval view of democracy serves

a certain liberal ideology, but it serves the opposite ideology even better. A former senior official of the Bush administration told me that "an efficient government is my worst nightmare. Let the wheels spin. . . . The only role of government," he perhaps overstated for rhetorical effect, "is to maintain a standing army." Process is extremely useful, he suggested, because it paralyzes government.

EPA's twenty-two-year delay in reviewing pesticides, a thousand diligent bureaucrats commuting in every morning and confronting impressive scientific studies, is just perpetual analysis. The pesticide makers, of course, like it that way; another decade of sales goes by before they have their day of judgment. According to pesticide expert Jim Aidala, who has now joined EPA to try to do something about it, "Nothing else presses the agency to make a decision; the data keeps coming in and nothing happens."

The Food and Drug Administration (FDA) is another example of what Professor Louis Jaffe called (aptly here) bureaucratic arteriosclerosis. There is one important difference. The industry needs FDA approval to go on the market with its products and is begging for decisions. But the result is the same: The FDA undertakes its important task of monitoring new drugs and medical devices with such caution that approvals for new drugs in America occur an average of six years after they've been approved by other Western countries. According to former FDA general counsel Peter Hutt, the FDA staffers never have to take responsibility: "They can just say, 'I'm not sure. Just do five more tests.'"

The FDA says it cannot be too careful. But there is also a cost to denying patients new pharmaceuticals. Professor Thomas Hazlett tells the story of trying to find treatment for his mother, who had terminal liver cancer. He was referred to a Harvard-trained researcher in Japan, who had conducted a ten-year trial of a drug that extended life expectancy of patients with advanced liver cancer up to six years. But the FDA had not approved it, and even though his mother would die in a matter of months, he could not buy the drug here or import it himself. Professor Hazlett had to place his mother in a Japanese hospital, "away from her house, her family and friends, her dog, her belongings." Then, after the treatment, she came back with a supply of her medicine. But no one in the U.S. was authorized to administer it. So Professor Hazlett had to drive her across the border to Mexico, a seven-hour round trip, several days every week.

The FDA will not take the chance that it might be criticized for approving a drug that has an unknown side effect. Administrators believe, perhaps correctly at this point, that American citizens will tolerate no risk. But in the meantime people are dying because they don't have the benefits of the new drugs. "To the patient," one observer has noted, "the impact may be the same if you deny good technology as if you allow bad technology on the market."

The average research cost of every new drug, two thirds of which goes to meeting FDA requirements, is $230 million (not a typographical error). One pharmaceutical company calculated that it spent more on forms and paperwork than it did on all research for cancer and other diseases. American citizens might be better served if all these funds were diverted to research in Japan and Germany, where more research would get accomplished and eventually trickle back to help cure disease in America.

But it is hard to criticize a system whose object, even if at the pace of evolution, is to find truth. With enough data and hearings, courts instructed us, correctness will peek out from the mountain of paper and reveal itself to the sore eyes of thousands of bureaucrats.

To Bazelon and most judges and lawyers, the purest form of process is our adversarial system, in which litigating lawyers make the best argument they can for their clients. You file a one-sided brief, and then I file one. But this procedure, as federal judge Henry Friendly once observed, is not designed for truth: "Under our adversary system the role of counsel is not to make sure the truth is ascertained but to advance his client's cause by any ethical means. . . . Causing delay and sowing confusion not only are his right but may be his duty."

Nor, as Judge Friendly concluded, is it useful as a tool for governing. Reality beats a quick retreat against the onslaught of argument. What seemed obvious becomes obscured in all the attention devoted to some point that one party decides to beat to death with thousands of pages or weeks of testimony. Scientific studies and opinions are easily dismissed by the trickery of the process. The National Academy of Sciences has pleaded for an end to this kind of decision making: "Confrontation and the adversary process do not create an atmosphere conducive to the careful weighing of scientific and technical knowledge, and distort the state of scientific and technical agreement and disagreement."

Agencies often have no idea what is going on. As Professor Gary Bryner has noted, "Regulatory agencies, often ignorant of the real positions of contending parties, are forced to guess at the priorities of each group."

Why doesn't the agency put its foot down on parties distorting science or stringing out the proceedings? Because that's not the philosophy: The agency is mainly a referee to the process, not a decision maker. This attitude, of course, only encourages more games. When agencies view themselves as a kind of passive oracle of the truth, the parties have little incentive to be moderate, or even intellectually honest. Process is the supreme value. As long as you abide by the rules, you can play all you want.

Charles Dickens would feel right at home. *Bleak House* portrayed a cynical, manipulative world of procedural intrigue, of lawyers manipulating court rules to guarantee, after decades of litigation, that the truth never emerges. It was a world in which every step was reasoned by the smartest legal minds and by impeccable logic flowing from the step that preceded it. The story of Jarndyce against Jarndyce is no more absurd than our government's pesticide review, twenty-two years of virtual inaction.

After all the hearings and handwringing, the decisions that emerge from agencies are rarely hailed for their correctness. "Public policy," former FDA counsel Peter Hutt concluded, "is inevitably controversial." He could not "recall one major safety decision . . . that failed to promote prolonged . . . public dispute." OSHA, after taking 105,000 pages of testimony, could not locate a solid factual consensus when creating a standard for cotton dust in the garment industry. The FDA, for all its caution, still approves products with defects and unknown side effects. Science, like everything else, involves judgment. Mistakes will always be made. Endless scrutiny does not necessarily make for a better judgment; the loss in perspective may well make for a worse judgment.

Notwithstanding all this purported fairness, most decisions are appealed in the courts, including 80 percent of EPA's decisions and 96 percent of OSHA's health standards. After years of bureaucratic paper-pushing, courts are presented with "gargantuan records, whose size," Judge Friendly observed, "varies inversely with usefulness." What the courts generally do is ignore the massive records and, after reviewing whatever the parties bring to their attention, make their own decision.

In 1984, for example, the Supreme Court overturned a Department of Transportation decision that no longer required automatic seat belts in cars. The agency had plenty of evidence that people just disconnected the seat belts anyway and, led by an elected laissez-faire president, it decided to scrap the rule. But the Supreme Court, elected by no one to make legislative-type decisions, decided to disagree by characterizing it as "arbitrary and capricious."

Court decisions in fact tend to be sensible, probably because only a couple of people are looking at the issue and can see the big picture. But then why do we need the grinding procedures for agencies? It might be more efficient for the bureaucrats to try to exercise common sense first. But this would require abandoning the pretense that one correct or best answer will emerge if the process is extensive enough. Announcing that this philosophy has no clothes requires no X-ray vision: Every decision depends on your point of view. What is right to a pesticide maker will not seem right to environmentalists. "Liberty for the wolves," the philosopher Isaiah Berlin noted, "is death for the lambs." The role of government is to make those choices, not to avoid them under the illusion of searching for nonexistent truth.

But the idea of getting to the right answer, even if hopeless, sounds right. So bureaucrats stare into the headlights of infinite information, transfixed by the brightness. Only with the greatest reluctance, under worldly pressures, do they turn around, half blinded, and look toward what might be illuminated. They surge forward and fall, en masse, onto a decision. Even Sherlock Holmes wouldn't be able to identify an actual decision maker. The process decided.

This is not an immutable feature of government. In the fall of 1982, seven people in the Chicago area died when cyanide was inserted into Tylenol packages. Other poisonings soon followed. In one month, the FDA issued final regulations for "tamper-resistant packaging" that affected upward of 400,000 products, and the crisis abated. Richard S. Schweiker, secretary of the Health and Human Services Department, said of the regulation: "We don't want to overreact; we don't want to underreact." He acknowledged, "It's not foolproof. You can counterfeit anything. The point is you just couldn't . . . fool anybody." This practical and expeditious approach, almost unique in recent regulatory history, required a national crisis.

In 1971, at a conference of prominent American and English jurists on administrative law, Lord Diplock concluded that "the main value from the English standpoint was to observe the horrible American examples . . . and to learn not to do likewise."

FIDDLING WHILE AMERICA FOUNDERS

Most citizens do not participate in these processes, and hear only the sweet music of procedural responsibility. Although angry at government's failures, we can close our eyes and take solace in the pure strains of process. Do you have a pet goal? Government will add it to the process. Most of us haven't yet made the connection that our bureaucratic crew is so busy playing procedural hymns that, like the band on the deck of the *Titanic*, it has given up trying to get anywhere.

Kings County Hospital sits in the middle of one of New York's poorest neighborhoods. Dilapidated and filled with antiquated equipment, it shoves people in and out of large wards that lack even rudimentary safeguards against the spread of infection. Some wings have no showers, and some floors have only one toilet for ten beds. The medical services offered in this largely minority community are embarrassingly inferior, and in 1984 the city budgeted $500 million to rebuild the hospital. It was expected that there would be as many as seven or eight main contractors, difficult to coordinate but necessary on a project of this size.

By February 1994, $120 million had been spent. But only two small administrative facilities had been built and the main excavation hadn't even begun. The number of contractors, however, had expanded prodigiously, from 7 to 110. "Our thinking," according to Ruth Bloom, a hospital board member, "was that it would be an opportunity for smaller businesses and minority companies to have a share." So the procedures were changed to satisfy, as *The New York Times* put it, "unrelated social and political goals." Nobody thought, said Ms. Bloom, that it would "actually cause a stalemate." The new head of the hospital agency, Dr. Bruce Siegel, stated the problem this way: "When you decide that finishing a project is not your first priority, then all sorts of problems happen. I think [the hospital] was on that slippery slope."

All of government is on that slippery slope. Turning the hospital construction project into a halfhearted affirmative action program ended up sabotaging both the hospital and the goal of helping minority businesses.

Without a clear goal in sight, process just spins on forever. In the Kings County Hospital project, the contract for digging and preparing the foundation, after years of delay, was awarded in April 1992. The lowest bidder was a company called Cross Bay. The second lowest bidder, Blandford, then came up with evidence that Cross Bay lacked "proper prequalification" under the agency's procedural rules. It also suggested that Cross Bay had a shady past. For over a year the excavation was held up by legal wrangling over whether Cross Bay had a pure background. Cross Bay was removed, then reinstated by a court, and then removed again. Then Blandford finally got the contract. In October 1993, Blandford was itself removed because undisclosed facts had been found in its past. In 1994 the bidding process was begun anew, presumably in the hope that an excavation company with evangelical inclinations could be found. What is the goal — to build a hospital or to save the souls of the construction industry? Why should bidders have any right to litigate over the character of other bidders? Reputation and honesty are important for practical reasons, but purity is not a common trait in the business world.

And how pure is pure? Sanctimony is the latest trend in judging government officials. Processes have been changed to make sure that all past sins are fully disclosed and then remain unforgiven. Within six months of John F. Kennedy's inauguration, he had made all his key appointments and his appointees were busy doing the work of his new administration. After a year in office, President Clinton still had hundreds of vacancies. The procedures required for confirmation — for example, detailing overseas travel in the prior fifteen years — make each approval tantamount to passing a new law. Potential presidential appointments generally arrive with a reputation. Is it really necessary to drive good people away from government, or to hold up all appointees, because the closet occasionally may contain a skeleton or (more likely) an untaxed diaper?

Setting priorities is difficult in modern government because process has no sense of priorities. Important, often urgent, projects get held up by procedural concerns. In 1993, during a snowstorm at New York's La Guardia Airport, a Continental Airlines DC-9 had to abort a takeoff and ended up with its nose in Long Island Sound. Another 100 feet and many lives would probably have been lost. Two years earlier, another plane had slid off the runway, killing 27 people. The 7,000-foot runway at La Guardia is about 70 percent as long as those at most commercial airports, and the Port Authority, which runs the airport, had been trying to add another 460 feet for six years. No one said no, but doing anything with water involves environmental issues, so nobody said yes either. Anxiety over the process, not the actual problem, was controlling the decisions. The Port Authority spent several years studying and negotiating with environmental agencies how it could mitigate any harmful effect in advance, and thereby avoid an environmental impact statement. Then, to head off possible private litigation, it spent several years in discussions with local citizens, promising, for example, a floating breakwater for a nearby marina. Mollifying individuals who might complain took precedence over making the airport safe.

On the other side of Manhattan, in Newark harbor, EPA stopped the Port Authority from its annual dredging for almost four years while it studied, and restudied, how to deal with mud that, as in many harbors, contains pollutants.

Newark's mud was found to contain small amounts of dioxin (less than ten parts per trillion), nothing to be ignored but not Chernobyl, either. Waiting for the decision was not benign: "In the meantime," noted a *Newsday* editorial, "the sediment is regularly churned up by ship propellers in the shallow harbor and the sea creatures absorb it," and "marine wildlife is being exposed to it."

Processes designed for public participation have also taken on a life of their own. In 1991, Donald Trump was persuaded by a coalition of civic groups (including one I am active in) to adopt a plan for developing a seventy-two-acre abandoned rail yard he owned on Manhattan's West Side. Arms locked together, this odd coalition of do-gooders and the Donald entered New York's three-level zoning-approval process. In total, our group attended over one hundred formal meetings, including twelve large public hearings, at which, I could (and did) testify, everyone said basically the same thing over and over. At the end of the process, an intense eighteen months later, the objectors sued. Their main grounds? After thousands of hours of meetings, they complained about the process — specifically, that one draft legal document had been provided six weeks later than certain others. They also said the environmental impact statement, almost two thousand pages long, was not complete. Our coalition won in court. But the project was held up another eighteen months for the litigation.

This was not the original point of participatory

democracy. In the New England town meeting, as Professor Martin Shapiro has noted, the idea is not that everyone be heard, but that everything is said that needs to be said.

All this governmental process has spilled over into our daily lives, and diverts us from doing our jobs. We fill out forms: Making sure everything is documented precisely is critical to modern process. Indeed, a tidal wave of forms has engulfed the country. Keeping up with OSHA's MSDS forms, like the ones caked with dust at the Glen-Gery Brick factory, takes 54 million hours per year. (At $20 per hour, that's about $1 billion to catalog the dangers of Windex and Joy.) Just by changing from monthly to yearly reporting on its school lunch program, the Department of Agriculture saved schools 9 million hours of paperwork. Under one environmental statute that requires extensive record keeping, 99.5 percent of all the covered chemicals are used by 14,000 companies; but 600,000 other companies, who use the other .5 percent of the chemicals, have to fill out all the same forms. As with detailed rules, "uniform procedures" have non-uniform effects.

The medical care industry is the hardest hit. Everything — every aspirin, every simple lab test — requires that a form be filled out. How else, the theory goes, can we assure that everything is in order? But hospitals now spend on the order of 25 percent of their budget on administration, mainly to comply with these procedural requirements. The machines that bind the forms at Columbia Presbyterian Hospital in New York City can no longer accommodate an average patient file. In the middle of a medical care crisis, it is unsettling to consider all the time spent by doctors, nurses, and staff on paperwork. Supposedly, the goal is to make sure that money isn't squandered, but the process itself squanders the money. Forty percent of all doctors say they would not choose the profession again, the main reason being "the 'hassle factor' — the growing levels of paperwork." It would not be that hard to reimburse and regulate by general categories. But such a system would not have perfect documentation of each incidental act.

It is as if some diabolical hater of government set all the reformers loose to build a perfect government, and they were so enamored of the utopian notions of democracy — searching for the one true answer, making sure every interest is fully heard, requiring every act to be documented by a form — that they lost sight of what it is government is supposed to be doing.

RITUAL AND CORRUPTION

Stamping out corruption, some believe, is worth any price. Multiple layers of procedure are the bulwark against breaches of the public trust. Does it work?

In 1986, a tip from a nervous collaborator exposed a scandal involving two prominent New York City politicians, Queens borough president Donald Manes and Bronx Democratic leader Stanley Friedman, and a city official named Geoffrey Lindenauer. The scam involved payoffs to get the contracts for providing, among other things, hand-held computers used when giving out parking tickets. Almost $1 million in bribes had been paid.

None of the people taking the bribes, however, had the authority to award the contracts. Elaborate safeguards had taken discretionary power away from individuals. Contracts could only be approved by vote of all key elected officials, after review and recommendation by every affected city agency. Extensive documentation accompanied each step.

In its report on the scandal, a blue ribbon panel led by Columbia University president Michael Sovern noted that the "documents on their face present a picture of a system of checks and balances designed to prevent any one person from unduly influencing the selection committee." Yet, looking back, "Geoffrey Lindenauer manipulated the system." The technique of Mr. Lindenauer was straightforward enough. He would attend the numerous meetings required under the procedures and, in various subtle ways, would indicate why the contracts seemed like a good idea. His only important lie was to say that he had seen a working model of the computers.

Mr. Lindenauer did not have authority to let

the contract. If he had, he would have been easier to catch. The problem was that no one had the authority to let the contract. In a system designed to discourage individual responsibility, a little encouragement goes a long way. Everyone, including the mayor, voted for it. The public, however, had no obvious official to blame. No one was asleep at the switch. Everyone was working hard to comply with the procedures. As the philosopher Hannah Arendt once observed about the explanation for Hitler's Germany, when everyone is guilty no one is guilty. The mayor's response to the scandal was just like the response of every other political leader faced with a scandal: He added more procedures.

On our scale of worst fears, corruption by government officials ranks, as best as I can guess, somewhere below dying and nudging up on infidelity. Mention the paring down of process to anyone and, quicker than a flash, you'll get a demand for "exceedingly tight controls," as Brookings' Herbert Kaufman put it in 1977. Fraud "eats away at the foundations of representative government," he cautioned, "so we are willing to put up with a lot to safeguard their integrity." Kaufman begrudgingly acknowledged that fraud happens anyway, but he concluded that without elaborate procedural checks and balances, there would "doubtless" be an epidemic of wrongdoing.

But who is accountable if no one has authority? Corruption and abuse, the Sovern Commission observed, "shun the bright light of day." It is not hard to slip something by in a system like New York City's, where a typical contract requires the approval of six agencies and produces paperwork that can be measured in pounds.

The paper trail of our endless procedures accomplishes nothing. Steven Kelman, in his study of federal computer procurement, quotes a former federal inspector-general, who concluded "that no matter how gross the corruption, one would still find the paperwork in order: 'You won't find anything in the documents.' "

In the late Roman empire, scandals also were answered by adding more layers of approval. Then, as now, officials with no clue of the facts dutifully placed their initials on piles of paper that were placed on their desks, with predictable effects: "The emperors and their ministers were so snowed under with papers that they signed them without reading them, and the clerks of the central ministries . . . could thus put through . . . illegal grants . . ."

The Defense Department scandals in 1988 show how easy it is to manipulate the system under modern procedures. Contracts worth billions of dollars were secured by bidders who bought information about the criteria to be used by the bureaucratic committees that were to let them. Kelman notes that while there was no opportunity to "throw a contract directly," all the contractors had to do was buy a little "inside information that allowed them to prepare better proposals."

Armed with this information, "they could present proposals that 'legitimately' made it through the formal procurement process and won the bids because they were indeed the best proposals, however corruptly designed." Kelman concludes that the elaborate federal procurement process "functions as a sort of Maginot line," which looks imposing but operates simply to redirect dishonesty into other areas.

Like the Maginot line, all these procedures provide a false sense of security. How could anything go wrong? Such an attitude, of course, is precisely what allows corruption to thrive. "Paradoxically," concluded one report, "too much control can have the same effect as too little." The dense red tape "has cloaked the entire contracting process and threatens the very integrity of the system it is designed to protect."

In 1988, a scandal embroiled the FDA. Guess what the payoffs were for? A generic drug company, Par Pharmaceutical, had paid bribes to cut through the procedural delays. What it wanted was not approval for its drugs, but merely to get near the front of the line for testing. Process came full circle; avoiding its inefficiencies is now an incentive for crime.

Until the 1970s, according to a study by Harvard's Kennedy School of Government, Hong Kong had a deeply embedded culture of corruption. The ideograms for the words *wealth* and *official position* are, indeed, the same in Cantonese. The police department was notorious for its venality, and the police commissioner had amassed tremendous wealth. Numerous efforts to clean up the corruption were unsuccessful until a new police commissioner decided that the way to cure the problem was to have less process.

Individual accountability was his goal. He persuaded the governor to eliminate most of the "cumbersome procedures" and "bureaucratic excess" that made it so difficult to do official business. By making it easier to deal with government, Hong Kong was able to reduce dramatically the opportunities for bribery. Hong Kong then focused on catching the crooks. Those dealing with government faced simpler decision making. Those working for government had to make decisions and be accountable for them and could not hide in the thicket of procedures. Hong Kong did not eliminate dishonesty, but it eliminated the culture of corruption.

Government officials, we keep forgetting, have no monopoly on dishonesty. Law deals with dishonesty everywhere. No society I can find has ever thought that the most effective way is to treat every citizen as a crook and impose an elaborate, mind-numbing, and demeaning ritual on every motion. Committees on committees, random drawings, rationalistic detail checked and double-checked, clear-cutting forests to print all the necessary forms and reports — these things do nothing except maybe hide the thievery. "Suspicion is itself never healthful," Woodrow Wilson said precisely in this context, "either in the private or in the public mind."

The common law has a system: It holds people accountable. But how would we do that? We could spend our energy trying to find the bad apples rather than assuming the worst of everyone. We do the opposite: Auditors are underfunded, and audits usually take two to four years longer than is acceptable. If we want to try to scare bureaucrats into honesty — contrary to Woodrow Wilson's advice that "trust is strength in all relations of life" — a Bureau of Accusations, Stings, and Humiliations (BASH) or the like would certainly be more frightening and a lot cheaper than the perpetual rituals we insist on now.

Plato argued that good people do not need laws to tell them to act responsibly, while bad people will always find a way around law. By pretending that procedure will get rid of corruption, we have succeeded only in humiliating honest people and provided a cover of darkness and complexity for the bad people. There is a scandal here, but it's not the result of venal bureaucrats.

A PLAYGROUND FOR MANIPULATION

Any ritual that has as its main purpose removing the authority and will of one side of a transaction has a predictable side effect. Government acts like a stupid giant, reacting always in lag time. Look over there (the pocket gets picked); look over here (the pollution pours out).

Taking advantage comes naturally when government can't easily do anything about it. Vendors play along with the government's rules, knowing full well that detailed contract specifications, like detailed rules, leave ample room for oversights. Even where the specifications are not defective, the detail will always provide loopholes. Contractors "bid in" at a low price and then (using the standard lingo) "get well" with very expensive change orders. The IRS regional office in California was shocked to receive a huge bill from a software vendor that had been the low bidder for supplying several IRS sites. The bill came to many times the amount agreed on. What's a "site"? The vendor interpreted "site" to mean not each IRS office but each computer station — i.e., each and every desk. The government paid up rather than litigate.

In New York City, as we have seen, the byzantine contract procedures drive most respectable bidders away; in one agency 75 percent of all contracts had only one or two bidders. The hardened core that is left often show up at auctions with two sealed envelopes, one with a competitive bid and one with something more like a winning lottery ticket. If no one else shows up, it's that vendor's lucky day. And we, the taxpayers, end up buying his beachfront condominium.

Process is easy. I have an image of a Washington lawyer yawning while leaning back in his armchair, instructing his associates to go get some more tests and file some more comments, knowing it will set the supervising agency back another nine months or so. For one pesticide, EPA received four thousand comments, all of which, under Judge Bazelon's rulings, it had to respond to. "Bureaucrats are overwhelmed," said Edward Fygi, general counsel of the Department of Energy. "The requirements impose savage competition on their time and attention."

Process has become the invincible secret weapon of the status quo. In 1984, after years of study, the Port of Oakland received the go-ahead to dredge its harbor. As in Newark harbor, finding a spot to which to move the mud was the main problem, except that the Oakland mud was not classified as hazardous. An area in the harbor near Alcatraz was the site of first choice, but locals objected and the state acceded to their complaints. A site fifteen miles into the ocean was then proposed, but fishing and environmental groups asserted that the environmental review process was inadequate and threatened to sue. Aware that a lawsuit would delay the project interminably, the Port agreed to move a small amount of mud to a spot thirty miles offshore and find another place for the rest. Another group of fishermen then sued, again based on inadequate process. Then a neighboring county sued, complaining about the process. The Port decided to look inland, and agreed with the City of Sacramento to transfer the mud there for use in dikes on the Sacramento River. Then a county downstream sued, claiming that the procedural review was inadequate. After six years, the project was on indefinite hold and the Port began losing tenants.

In 1993, limited dredging was permitted to keep the Port of Oakland working. As of mid-1994, after $25 million has been spent on studies, the review process continues. The latest idea is to scrape away a golf course, put the mud there, and then make another golf course.

Professor Robert Kagan has chronicled the Oakland story as an example of how "adversarial legalism" has made it nearly impossible for government to act. I have a slightly different take: You can't fight process, at least not with any confidence. It's too vague, and has no natural closure. Someone else can always complain that the process isn't fair to him. If the Oakland fight had hinged on whether the dumping itself (as opposed to the process) was reasonable, then the Port could have taken its stand in court and won or lost.

Environmental review procedures were instituted with the intent of ensuring responsible decision making. Instead, they have transferred power, supposedly lodged in democratically elected officials, to private groups or to next-door neighbors, who can stall anything on procedural nit-picking or, sometimes, just on the threat of invoking the claim. Joe Riley, the mayor of Charleston, South Carolina, spoke to me with obvious frustration about his numerous encounters with the environmental review process: "The process ends up empowering a lot of people. They don't have to win. No burden of proof at all. All they need is a point. And they hold on to it for eighteen months and the project is dead."

Government doesn't seem to mind that process has taken away its authority. When the Supreme Court blocked the highway in Memphis at the request of the Citizens to Preserve Overton Park, Congress did not stand up and object that the environmental impact statement was being misused as a blocking device. From Congress's standpoint, the result was perfect: What could be better in a tough environmental issue than allowing the adversaries to slug it out in the courts? But is that really what we want from government?

Manipulation of process tends to become easier as the amount at stake goes down. Trying to get rid of an inept federal employee, for example, is so difficult that most supervisors don't try. According to a recent Government Accounting Office report, "it is not worth the time and effort for supervisors to pursue that course of action. . . . The easiest approach (and one proven successfully by other supervisors) [is] to ignore the problem and assign any essential work to other employees."

With extensive process always standing as a high wall between them and accountability, what people can get away with is pretty remarkable. For fourteen years, John Nesbit was an assistant United States attorney, and at the end of his service he was the chief of his unit. The head of his division had a secretary, call her Ms. Jones, whose "dedication to her work was nil." The division head couldn't take her anymore and took the low road: He reassigned her to his two unit chiefs, including Mr. Nesbit. They decided to tackle the problem head-on: She was told she had to come to work on time. She ignored them. They began keeping records on her absences. When her annual review came up, their comments called for a "serious downgrade" of her level of performance.

Ms. Jones demanded an arbitration over her job review. She hired a lawyer. She also filed a discrimination claim. In the peculiar world of civil service, the supervisor has the burden of proving, in a formal hearing, that his judgment is valid. Several months later, after the hearing, Ms. Jones lost. As everyone in the office knew, Ms. Jones was not doing her job. The result? Ms. Jones got a lower than usual raise, the only penalty for a "serious downgrade." No one had the authority to fire her; that would have taken years.

A few months after the arbitration, Ms. Jones was assigned one afternoon to help a junior lawyer with an emergency application. An hour later, the lawyer walked by and noticed Ms. Jones, obviously on a social call, not doing the work. She reminded Ms. Jones that the job had to be done immediately. Ms. Jones stayed on the phone. A few minutes later Ms. Jones, an imposing figure, walked into the lawyer's office and, shaking her finger in the lawyer's face, said that if the lawyer ever interrupted her again, she was going to "kick her ass." The lawyer, outraged, complained to the head of personnel, who recommended a warning. The lawyer, more outraged, demanded disciplinary action. The personnel office responded, under the procedures, by appointing an investigator and putting Ms. Jones on paid leave. By the time the investigator got around to looking into the incident, nine months had passed. The other members of the staff were furious: Misconduct gets you a paid vacation.

During this period, another lawyer from the office was interviewing for a job at a law firm and ran into Ms. Jones. She was working somewhere else while the federal government investigated her conduct and paid her salary. Process rewards those who know its power.

Society at large is catching on. Recently, posters were spotted on the Upper West Side in Manhattan seeking a credit-worthy person to share an apartment rent-free. The plan, detailed on the poster, was to sign a lease, move in, and then refuse to pay rent. Under New York City procedures, the poster explained, a minimum of eighteen months is required for the landlord to get an order of eviction. So, thanks to the cost of process, you can live free and move on.

In 1993, a New York City Transit bus was hit by a garbage truck on 125th Street. Within a month, eighteen people filed lawsuits against the city, claiming injuries received when they were hurled down in the bus. The accident was not caused because the bus driver was diverted by the allure of a quarter that had just gotten jammed in the fare box. There were no coins in the box; indeed, no passengers were on the bus. The bus had gone out of service and was parked. But the eighteen claimants did not know that. They all claimed they had been passengers and had hobbled on home before the police arrived. Their scam, which often succeeds, was the result of their knowing that the city would typically settle rather than bear the expense of trying to prove they weren't there.

The ransom available by invoking process has become so common as to be generally accepted. Tycoons play a similar game, frequently using legal processes as a device to stall an adversary; it is not fraud, of course, just misuse of law to serve an ulterior purpose.

The irony cannot be allowed to pass: Process was intended to make sure everything was done responsibly. It has instead become a device for manipulation, even extortion.

THE PROCESS PARADOX

Only because our devotion to process is so un-questioning have we been able to endure paradoxes that, like leeches on a weakening patient, steadily drain our vitality. Stupendous waste in the name of neutral efficiency is only the most obvious of these paradoxes. Lobotomizing bureaucrats and expecting better results is another. Treating every public employee like a crook while avoiding rudimentary precautions like audits is another. Failing to protect us against industrial poisons by claiming to analyze them perfectly is another.

Government cannot accomplish anything when multiple procedures are required for almost every decision. The New Deal was able to act only because it used all-new agencies that had no elaborate procedures in place. During the same period the accumulated procedures of the Interstate Commerce Commission, which had been in business for four decades, made that agency as inefficient as ever. Governor Nelson Rockefeller of New York got around heavy bureaucracies for his massive building program by creating a new agency, the Urban Development Corporation, with broad powers to override other agencies' procedures. *Reinventing Government* preaches the credo of flexibility without emphasizing the cold truth that flexibility only comes from abandoning the procedural orthodoxy on which modern government is now built.

An unworkable contradiction lies at the heart of the modern state. Process is a defensive device; the more procedures, the less government can do. We demand an activist government while also demanding elaborate procedural protections against government. We have our foot heavy on the accelerator, seeking government's help in areas like guarding the environment. Simultaneously, we have stomped hard on the brake, refusing to allow any action except after nearly endless layers of procedure.

Process is an ethereal concept, difficult to grab on to or to even think about changing. We know it makes us unable to keep sight of our goals, like a fog, but how do we part it? Focusing is a useful first step: The route to a public goal cannot be diverted through endless switchbacks of other public goals, for example, without losing sight of the original destination. But we will never clear away the procedural fog until we redefine our values. Which is more important: the process or the result? In answering this question, it is useful to reexamine the core assumption that the primacy of process is essential to a fair and responsible government.

THE REAL UNFAIRNESS OF PROCEDURAL FAIRNESS

The Abyssinian Baptist Church in Harlem runs a not-for-profit housing corporation that builds about a hundred units of low-cost housing a year. Several years ago it approached New York City with the idea of fixing up two buildings across the street from the church. The city liked the idea but said that, under its procedures, it couldn't just negotiate with the church; that would be favoritism. After six months or so, the city put out a request for proposals (commonly known as an RFP), but according to Rev. Calvin Butts, the terms were not realistic: "We knew more work was required to make the buildings habitable, but the city wouldn't talk. They had already prepared their RFP." Another developer, not from the neighborhood, put in a bid and got the contract. "Sure enough," said Rev. Butts, "the improvements didn't work very well, and guess who they're looking to now."

Rev. Butts says that he doesn't object to the idea of competitive bids, but "they ought to value our reputation and reliability. We do over a hundred units a year. They know who we are. The church has been in New York for 180 years. We're not going anyplace. If we do a bad job, they know where to find us. Why doesn't that count?" When asked what he could do without all the procedures, Rev. Butts paused, then said quietly: "If we could sit down with the city and have an ordinary negotiation, we could easily build twice the number of units. And I assure you, it would cost a lot less."

Procedures pay allegiance to the idea of uniform fairness. But is it really fair to assume that the Abyssinian Baptist Church is the same as some unknown bidder? Fair to whom?

Rote devotion to sameness is not necessarily the same as responsibility in government. Many people might prefer government to help Rev. Butts build a strong neighborhood, not to make every decision under a green eyeshade in the name of the antiseptic fairness that Max Weber described. Is the out-of-towner the "same" as the person with a commitment to the neighborhood? So what if this involves a value judgment? Isn't this the only kind of judgment that makes sense? Democracy is not intended to purge our values but to reflect them.

Steven Kelman has noted the perversities of a "fair" system in which vendors who do a good job get no credit and every new contract must be bid separately without the "favoritism" of recognizing a job well done. Should someone who does a good job be treated "the same" as someone who did a bad job? There can be "no rational administration of government," the Greek historian Polybius once said, "when good men are held in the same esteem as bad ones."

But, you might ask, doesn't government have to treat everyone the same? Actually, aside from basic services, government seems to be in the business of treating people differently. Congress sits there practically every day figuring out how it can do special things for people. It compensates rich homeowners who built on beaches and were surprised at nature's nerve; it spends $2 billion subsidizing sugarcane producers for reasons I can't understand; it gives the Irish special treatment in immigration for reasons I can at least attribute to someone; it doles out foreign aid but gives none (at least not recently) to Iraq. All these things can be called favoritism; they are all redressable — not in court, but at the ballot box.

How does this fit in with the Constitution? Well,

government can't coerce anyone without due process, but building low-income housing is not coercion. It's just a business that government is in for our common benefit. Bureaucracy is not a court but an arm of government with a job to do. It should be professional and effective, not pretend it is minding the gates of heaven.

The governing part of government, you already know, has to be different. Surely, equality requires a uniform fairness when government is regulating. But, again, what is fairness? Is it fairness only to the person being regulated, or is it also fairness to the common good? Fairness in the regulatory process is not a one-sided concept: The pesticide manufacturer and the oil refinery are putting poisons on our food and into our air. The process should reflect the reality, as Professor Richard Stewart has noted, that "the distinct spheres of private and governmental activity have melded."

Instilling pragmatism into process requires no break from democratic traditions. Calling off the debate after a few months (instead of a few decades), for example, involves no unfairness. Constitutional rights are not violated when courts limit the evidence and restrict parties to two briefs each. "Delay," as New Dealer Jim Landis once said, "is equally an element of the lack of due process" as barring the courthouse door is. We're the ones ingesting the pesticides and breathing the benzene, and we're entitled to a decision.

Procedural fairness sounds good, but it turns out to be troubling in action. It so quickly spins out of reality: Dredging the harbor is debated not on its environmental impact but on whether the disclosure statement was free from quibble; the employee who misbehaves puts the supervisor on the defensive by referring to the procedures.

Is the modern ideal of procedural fairness fair to the common good? I don't think so. Maybe it is "fair" to individuals who want to take advantage of government. But who does government think it's working for, some unknown vendor or all the taxpayers? Maybe we should vote on it.

"Practically everyone has lost respect for the regulatory process," says Professor Richard Stewart. How could it be otherwise, with the delays, the costs, the manipulations, the hypocrisy, and, perhaps worst, the boasts of a fairness that destroys real fairness?

REMEMBERING RESPONSIBILITY

Sam Schwartz is not likely to make it into the annals of history for fixing up the Carroll Street Bridge in time for a centennial party. But he got the job done. Nor does it offend you, I bet, that he violated every rule in the book. The reason is that he was willing to put himself on the line and take responsibility. That is why the job got done. Responsibility, not process, is the key ingredient to action.

As we have developed process into a kind of religion in recent decades, we thought that the more people there were who took responsibility, the better off we would be. Responsibility, however, is not a group concept. As Friedrich Hayek once suggested, sharing responsibility widely, like sharing property widely, is like having no responsibility at all.

We stole the idea of avoiding individual judgment from the rationalists, not very cleverly adopting a version of central planning at the height of the cold war. The dream of an automatic government, liberated from the perils of human choice, fit neatly with our traditional fear of government. It sounded perfect: Government would regulate and provide services without its officials having to think. It is too perfect. It is utopian and, as Isaiah Berlin warned, our "determined effort to produce it" by erecting a huge monument of rules and elaborate rituals of process has led to "suffering, disillusionment and failure."

To Jim Landis, an effective government was one that attracts the best possible people and gives them leadership responsibility. We have created the opposite system, one profoundly focused on the negative, obsessed with defensive formalisms and driving away good people who cannot, to quote John Rollwagon, "grow the gills" needed to breathe in this underworld of process.

We must remember why we have process at all. Process exists only to serve responsibility. Process was not a credit card given out to each citizen for misconduct or delay; nor was it an invisible shield given to each bureaucrat. Take the most extreme case: Due process is not a weapon handed out to criminals. Our founders weren't saying, "Go out and see what you can get away with. We'll tie one hand behind our backs." Our founders were concerned about the irresponsible use of government power. Responsibility is what matters. Process is only one of many tools to get there.

III

A Nation of
Enemies

F inding a public bathroom in New York City is not easy. Most subway toilets were closed down years ago because of vandalism and crime. Museums require people to pay admission. Restaurant bathrooms are restricted to patrons' use. As public toilets became scarce, the nooks and crannies around the city began to exude the malodorous costs of this shortage. "No one needed to be told that this was a serious problem," observed Joan Davidson, a director of a private foundation, the J. M. Kaplan Fund.

Ms. Davidson was nonetheless surprised at the outpouring of enthusiasm when, in 1991, the Kaplan Fund put forward a modest proposal to finance a test of six sidewalk toilet kiosks in different sections of the city. The coin-operated toilets would be imported from Paris, where the municipal government provides them for the convenience of residents and tourists. Perfected over years of experience in Paris, these facilities were almost too good to be true. They clean themselves with a shower of water and disinfectant after each use. The doors open automatically after fifteen minutes so they cannot be used as a place to spend the night. They are small, only five feet in diameter, which means that New York's crowded sidewalks would not be blocked. And while the City of Paris rents them, they would cost budget-strapped New York nothing: Advertising panels would be added on the outside to pay the freight. City Hall was ready to move. The six-month test, in sites from Harlem down to City Hall, would show whether they would work in New York.

Then came the glitch. Wheelchairs couldn't fit inside them. New York's antidiscrimination law provides that it is illegal to "withhold or deny" from the disabled any access to "public accommodation." Ann Emerman, the head of the Mayor's Office of the Disabled, characterized the sidewalk toilet proposal as "discrimination in its purest form." When the city's chief lawyer, Victor Kovner, whose credentials as a champion of liberal causes stretch back thirty years, sought a legislative amendment to permit the six-month test, another lobbyist for the disabled accused him of "conspiring to violate the law." Never mind that he was seeking to amend the law through the democratic process.

Suggestions that disabled-accessible bathrooms might be provided in nearby buildings or restaurants were dismissed out-of-hand: "The law requires that everyone go to the bathroom in exactly the same place." When someone had the nerve, at a public forum, to ask how many wheelchair users there might be compared with other citizens who might benefit (including blind and deaf citizens), the questioner was hooted down for asking a politically incorrect question. At stake, at least for the disabled, were their "rights." When you have a right to something, it doesn't matter what anyone thinks or whether you are, in fact, reasonable.

A kiosk accommodating wheelchairs had in fact been tried in both London and Paris, but it had to be much larger and, because of its size, it could be placed only in locations where there was ample pedestrian room. Also, it was not self-cleaning. Because of the different needs of wheel-chair users, it would not self-open until after thirty minutes, and experience showed that it became a refuge for prostitution and drug use. The lobby for the disabled demanded this larger kiosk or nothing.

Good-government groups and editorial boards were livid at the selfishness and intractability of the lobby. The leaders of the disabled lobby, who refer to the general public as the "temporarily abled," cast us as shortsighted bigots. Compromise was unthinkable. Politicians, ever eager to please, ducked for cover.

The ultimate resolution, while arguably legal, was undeniably silly: Two toilet kiosks would be at each of three locations, one for the general public and another, with a full-time attendant, available only for wheelchair users. Mrs. Emerman and other advocates for the disabled were still upset. Their credo is "mainstreaming": the legal right to do everything in the same way as everyone else. They still wanted the disabled to use the same toilet — not one made specifically for them — or wanted no toilet for anyone.

The test proved how great the demand was in New York. The regular units averaged over three thousand flushes per month, or 50 percent more than the average in Paris. The larger units reserved for the disabled were basically unused, the cost of the full-time attendant wasted. The test also made enemies of everyone; even liberals who had championed the cause of the disabled began to see their advocates as unreasonable zealots.

Making trade-offs in situations like this is much of what government does: Almost every government act, whether allocating use of public property, creating new programs, or granting subsidies, benefits one group more than another, and usually at the expense of everyone else. Most people expect their elected and appointed leaders to balance the pros and cons and make decisions in the public interest. The government of New York, however, lacked this power, because it had passed an innocuous-sounding law that created "rights" elevating the interests of any disabled person over any other public purpose.

Rights, almost no one needs to be told, are all around us. The language of rights is used everywhere in modern America — not only in public life, but in the workplace, in school, in welfare offices, in health care. There are rights for children and the elderly; the disabled; the mentally

154

disabled; workers under twenty-five and over forty; alcoholics and the addicted; the homeless; spotted owls and snail darters.

Rights are considered as American as apple pie. This is a country where citizens have *rights*. The Bill of Rights is the best-known part of the Constitution: Government can't tell us what to say, and can't take away our "life, liberty or property" except by due process. Rights are basic. Until the last few decades, however, rights were not something to shout about. They were the bedrock of our society, something we would give our lives to defend, but not something people thought much about as they made it through each day. Rights were synonymous with freedom, protection against being ordered around by government or others.

Rights have taken on a new role in America. Whenever there is a perceived injustice, new rights are created to help the victims. These rights are different: While the rights-bearers may see them as "protection," they don't protect so much as provide. These rights are intended as a new, and often invisible, form of subsidy. They are provided at everyone else's expense, but the amount of the check is left blank. For example, in New York, the unintended consequence of giving the disabled the "right" to do everything in the same way was the imposition of a de facto prohibition of sidewalk toilets.

Handing out rights like land grants has become the preferred method of staking out a place for those who feel disadvantaged. Lawmakers and courts, confronted with evidence of past abuses, scramble over each other to define and take credit for handing out new rights. When refused entry to a movie because his two-year-old son might disturb the other patrons, Rolando Acosta, then deputy commissioner of New York City's Human Rights Commission, had an easy fix; the commission ruled that banning children was age discrimination. In 1993, a judge in Rhode Island found rights for obese employees. Mari Matsuda, a feminist legal scholar, has advocated rights for those who are discriminated against on account of unusual accents — people who talk differently would be able to sue if they feel their accent is being held against them. In 1990, the federal government enacted a comprehensive disabled law, the Americans with Disabilities Act (known as the ADA), to serve similar purposes as New York's. "Let the shameful wall of exclusion finally come tumbling down," said President Bush on the South Lawn of the White House upon signing the bill. The law had passed with virtually no opposition. After all, rights cost little or nothing out of the budget. It's only a matter of being fair. Or so we think.

Rights, however, leave no room for balance, or for looking at it from everybody's point of view as well. Rights, as the legal philosopher Ronald Dworkin has noted, are a trump card. Rights give open-ended power to one group, and it comes out of everybody else's hide. What about the three hundred other moviegoers when the two-year-old starts crying or demanding candy in a loud voice? Too bad; we gave children a right. Rights cede control to those least likely to use them wisely, usually partisans like disabled activists who have devoted their lives to remedying their own injustices. Government, for all its flaws, at least has interest in a balanced result.

This abdication has led to an inverted feudalism in which the rights-bearer, by assertion of legal and moral superiority, lords it over everyone else. Rights-bearers do warfare independent of the constraints of democracy: *Give Us Our Rights*. We cringe, lacking even a vocabulary to respond.

It was only three decades ago that John F. Kennedy stirred the nation when, in his inaugural address, he said, "Ask not what your country can do for you, but what you can do for your country." Thirty years later, we have disintegrated into factions preoccupied only with our due, not what we can do.

What went wrong?

THE GREAT RIGHTS RUSH

Tocqueville observed that the period of productive reform is often also the most dangerous for a society:

> The most perilous moment for a bad government is one when it seeks to mend its

ways . . . For the mere fact that certain abuses have been remedied draws attention to the others and they now appear more galling; people may suffer less, but their sensibility is exacerbated.

It seems like ancient history, but barely forty years ago segregation of blacks was required by law in certain states. Women, trapped in a different cage, were offered labor-saving appliances as the key to fulfillment. Even an ardent sexist would grimace when reminded that Supreme Court justice Sandra Day O'Connor, after graduating at the top of her class at Stanford Law School in 1952, couldn't find a job in San Francisco.

The 1950s American dream, with its ranch houses and cars with tail fins, was not decadent: It was optimistic, even buoyant. Our country had just finished two decades of struggling to overcome the Depression and the worst villain in history. We aspired to decent values of hard work and community.

Our collective gaze, however, had been trained not to notice the victims of injustice and neglect that were all around us. Racism had been accepted for centuries. Sexism, a term that would have been almost incomprehensible in the 1950s, reached back millennia. Mental patients were locked up in institutions and largely forgotten. What were known as retarded children had little or no support from local school systems. People in wheelchairs often wasted away at home. Gays were securely locked in the closet. The "environment" was not known as such, but lakes and rivers were getting filthy.

Some people began looking around and asking why these conditions existed in a heroic and enlightened society. But our frame of reference, including racism and neglect, had been accepted for so long that a mighty heave was required to dislodge it. As Tocqueville warned, however, the momentum was likely to carry it to a point where the values that prompted the reform were themselves eroded. Something similar has happened to us. Freedom is now confused with power: "You must do this for me" has replaced "We should all be free."

Seeking balance has become difficult because we have misplaced the vocabulary of accommodation. Indeed, we seem to have forgotten why accommodation was ever necessary. The idea of weighing priorities has somehow become un-American. Unless something is done, the forces of change will be reversed, with the aid of Rush Limbaugh and others, with equal force. "Let's fight" is the increasingly common response to "It's my right."

The "rights revolution" did not begin with any of this in mind. It was an effort to give to blacks the freedom that all the rest of us enjoyed. The landmark 1954 Supreme Court decision of *Brown v. Board of Education* overturned laws mandating "separate but equal" public schools. Other decisions soon applied the *Brown* ruling to other public facilities: Southern states, having been given a clear mandate by the United States Supreme Court, then proceeded to ignore it. Prince Edward County, Virginia, for example, closed down its public schools and the municipal swimming pool rather than integrate.

Fed up, Congress in 1964 passed the Civil Rights Act. The most controversial part, known as Title II, banned segregation in private establishments that accommodated the public, such as restaurants, movie theaters, and hotels. One southern hotel, under a court injunction, burned the sheets after the stay of each black guest. The better-known practice of southern dissidents was to wear the sheets. Parts of the South were almost at war.

Although it is strange to recall it today, a shopkeeper's refusal to serve blacks had been considered a prerogative similar to choosing who comes into your home. Looking at it as legal history, Title II represented a constitutional break not unlike the fight over the supremacy of states' rights that led to the Civil War. However, while opening the doors of restaurants didn't go down easy, ultimately it wasn't hard to enforce: A paying customer is a paying customer. By the 1970s the conflict over Title II had largely ended.

Dealing with workplace discrimination, prohibited by Title VII of the act, was more complicated. Every worker is different, and assessing skills and attitudes requires subjective evaluation. Seniority rules confused the issue of promotion: Is it fair to make blacks and women start at the bottom? Is it fair to bump a white male who has put in twenty good years? Where discrimination patterns were obvious — for example, where a business refused to interview and hire blacks — courts could easily intervene. Beyond the obvious discrimination patterns, no one thought much about how the law would work.

The ban against gender discrimination was inserted in the Civil Rights Act almost as a joke, offered by Rep. Howard Smith of Virginia "in the spirit of satire and ironic cajolery" to try to sabotage the bill. There was no women's right movement lobbying for it. It exists today, as perhaps the most significant law for women, only because everyone ignored Smith's ploy.

Title VII didn't require anyone to *do* anything. Like the Bill of Rights, it was written in the negative. It forbade discrimination, based on "race, color, sex, religion or national origin." Title VII said that you could not be denied a job because of your status, but it did not create affirmative rights: You couldn't demand a job *because* you were black or a woman.

The defensive posture of Title VII was emphasized by its legislative sponsors. To Senator Harrison Williams equality, not special power, was the goal:

How can the language of equality favor one race or one religion or another? Equality can have only one meaning, and that meaning is self-evident to reasonable men. Those who say that equality means favoritism do violence to common sense.

Senator Hubert Humphrey made clear that the act did not require anyone to act affirmatively:

If [anyone] can find in Title VII . . . any language which provide[s] that an employer will have to hire on the basis of percentage or quota related to color, race, religion or national origin, I will start eating the pages one after another, because it is not in there.

The senators' caution against special powers reflected a fear about rights almost forgotten today, and in fact forgotten before the end of the 1960s. They knew that in legislating rights, they were stepping outside the traditional bounds of Congress. Rights were not the language of government action. Rights were the protections that prevented government and others from telling us what we could say, where we could travel, or who our friends could be. "Rights," said Oliver Wendell Holmes, "mark the limits of interference with individual freedom."

The business of government was conducted using not the language of rights but of legal obligation. Leaving aside the rhetoric, all the social engineering of the New Deal — welfare, Social Security, job programs — was done without creating broad-based "rights."

To be fair, the lines easily blur. If someone has an obligation to you, you naturally talk of having a right. A philosopher will say that rights and obligations are two sides of the same coin. But obligations tend to be limited, because the politics of spending money, or of telling people what to do, impose a natural limit on how far a legislature can go. Rights, in the sense that most people understand them, convey open-ended powers. They belong to the rights-bearers, like owning a kind of intangible property. Rights have a beneficent ring, as if they ensure justice without cost. But the cost becomes quickly apparent as rights are asserted.

The adoption of the word *rights* in the civil rights movement was unusual, but it was also appropriate, because it did indeed invoke rights of constitutional dimension — the rights of freedom — that an entire segment of the population had been deprived of. The Civil Rights Act was defended as a shield of freedom, a protection against interference by racists. No John C. Calhoun was required, however, to see it exactly the opposite way — that basic freedoms of bigots to deal with whom they wished were being abridged.

The Civil Rights Act broke huge holes through barriers of employment discrimination that had stood for centuries. In industry after industry, either voluntarily or by class-action suits, blacks and then women were admitted into areas of en-

163

deavor where they had never been allowed. By 1980, most obvious barriers were down and affirmative action offices were commonplace. No one claimed that prejudice had disappeared. Martin Luther King, Jr., for one, always knew that while law could mandate desegregation, a change in spirit, not law, was required to achieve the "democratic dream of integration." But legislating new rights had worked to accomplish a radical change in society.

As centuries of discrimination began to break down under a simple mandate of civil rights law, reformers thought they were witnessing a miracle. Like the Progressives at the turn of the century who tried to turn law into a science, reformers in the 1960s and 1970s began to advocate a wholesale change in the way law worked. Why not use "rights" as a method to eliminate inequality altogether? To the reformers, the special nature of racial discrimination did not seem important. After all, "rights" seemed to be working also for women. Reformers zeroed in on the almost nuclear power that "rights" could bring to their causes. People armed with new rights could solve their own problems by going straight to court, bypassing the maddeningly slow processes of democracy.

The most influential thinker was Charles Reich, at Yale. In his 1964 article "The New Property," Reich laid out a simple formula to empower the citizens: Government decisions should be considered, in essence, the property of the people affected. Government employees facing termination, professionals licensed by the state, and contractors doing government business no longer would be subject to the judgment of government officials. Everyone would have a "right" that government would have no choice but to respect. "Government should gain no power," Reich asserted, "by reason of its role as a dispenser of wealth."

Legislatures, according to Reich, often have "a simplistic notion of the public interest" that can "undermine the independence of the individual":

> From the individual's point of view, it is not any particular kind of power, but all kinds of power, that are to be feared. This is the lesson of the public interest state. . . . Liberty is the right to defy the majority and to do what is unreasonable.

A startling paradox underlay Reich's thesis: It was a combination platter of libertarian freedom and socialist benefits. Why have a public interest state if you do not want it to make reasonable judgments in the public interest? How can government sensibly allocate benefits if it must jump through hoops to override the selfish demands of each citizen? Authority was flipped upside down. Government would be like a rich uncle under your personal control.

In a follow-up article the next year, Reich focused on what he thought, correctly, was the area in which government largess was most important to the individual: welfare. His evaluation of the problem was unambiguous: "subjecting large numbers of people to bureaucratic discretion." His solution was equally unambiguous — a new "bill of rights for the disinherited." His vision heralded a new era of self-determination. Power would be transferred to the wards of the welfare state. Reich's ideas seemed admirable, almost utopian. But who would draw the line? Reich himself knew that he was lighting a bonfire: "Lawyers," he proclaimed, "are desperately needed now."

Reich got his wish. Today, even ordinary human encounters — between teachers and students, between supervisors and employees — often involve lawyers. It started slowly enough, but it proved to be difficult to stop. Like termites eating their way through a home, "rights" began weakening the lines of authority of our society. Traditional walls of responsibility — how a teacher manages a classroom or how a social worker makes judgments in the field — began to weaken.

Every generation has its injustices and its reforms. What was novel about the period beginning in the mid-1960s was that the reflexive solution was to hand out rights. Rights became a fad.

Congress pressed forward against discrimination. In 1967, to "promote employment of older persons based on their abilities rather than age," Congress passed the Age Discrimination of Employment Act (ADEA), giving workers over forty the right to sue for "age discrimination." In hindsight, it was like a formula for discrimination stalemate: How could protecting the place of older white males help but shut out minorities and women trying to break into all-male, all-white bastions? No one even asked the question.

After thirty years of expanding rights against workplace discrimination, Congress has succeeded in "protecting" over 70 percent of all American workers. In many states that legislate their own rights, practically everyone can now sue for discrimination. Whom, one might ask, are they being protected against? Many people have multiple potential claims: an Asian woman over forty with a physical ailment, like a bad back, enjoys four protections. Aaron Wildavsky calculated that if you apply all the protected categories, they add up to 374 percent of the American population. Only one group has no protection against employment discrimination: employees of Congress.

The Supreme Court embraced Professor Reich's concept of rights in a 1970 decision, *Goldberg* v. *Kelly*, which held that welfare benefits were "property" within the meaning of the Constitution and could not be cut off without due process. Due process doesn't sound like much, but now government had to worry about a court always looking over its shoulder to see if every *i* was dotted. To the rights-bearer, due process implies ownership and entitlement. To the government, it breeds formalism and defensiveness: Every judgment must be backed up by piles of forms.

Juvenile justice was turned upside down. Reformers of an earlier generation had created an informal system for juvenile offenders in which, without the rigid procedures and harsh associations of the adult criminal world, teenagers could be worked with, not just prosecuted at arm's length. As Jane Addams wrote in 1935:

> [W]hen the Juvenile Court was established
> . . . the child was brought before the judge
> with no one to prosecute him and with no
> one to defend him — the judge and all concerned were merely trying to find out what
> could be done on his behalf.

But a system permitting understanding and flexibility, even if it works better in nineteen out of twenty cases, also carries with it the opportunity for abuse. In 1964, Gerald Gault, a fifteen-year-old, was arrested at his home in Arizona for making an obscene phone call and, without being told of the consequences or having a chance to talk to a lawyer, confessed to doing it. He was sent to a reformatory for up to six years, an absurdly harsh penalty for an infraction that, for an adult, carried a fifty-dollar fine and a maximum two-month sentence. Faced with glaring injustice, the Supreme Court held broadly that due process of criminal courts must also be applied to juvenile courts: "Under our Constitution," pronounced the Court, "the condition of being a boy does not justify a kangaroo court."

The undeniable evil of a kangaroo court, however, does not necessarily lead to the conclusion that juvenile courts should abandon hard-fought-for reforms and revert to a formalistic system. Why not just correct the injustice in that case?

Due process had never been considered relevant in situations pertaining to teachers and classrooms. With "rights" in the air, however, due process had no trouble making the short trip from juvenile justice to public schools. As usual, the first case involved an aberrational event. Five students in Des Moines, Iowa, were suspended from school for wearing black armbands in protest of the Vietnam War. In stentorian tones the Supreme Court in 1969 declared, "Students don't check their rights at the front door."

In 1975, in Columbus, Ohio, several students were suspended for a "lunchroom disturbance" involving a political sit-in. The discipline was meted out by the principal, who witnessed the incident. The Supreme Court overturned the suspensions, relying explicitly on Charles Reich's formulation: Students had a property right to their own education, and although the principal saw the entire event, he had not afforded them the hearings of due process. The amount of due process that was due, the Supreme Court explained, would depend on the interest at stake, and did not necessarily require trial-type protections.

But how does a principal know how much process is required? Is a meeting in the principal's office sufficient? A hearing? A right to witnesses and cross-examination? Phoning up the Supreme Court to determine how much due process is due is, unfortunately, not a service yet available. Teachers and principals confronting disciplinary decisions were left to guess at the contours of future constitutional rulings. And then, in the same year, the Court ruled that school officials who had suspended two sixteen-year-olds for three months for spiking the punch at a school function in Arkansas (it was a dry county) could be personally sued for violating their due process.

Faced with a sliding scale of due process that was undefinable, and with the right of students to sue any school official who "knew or reasonably should have known" that he was violating a student's constitutional rights, school officials reacted predictably. Almost overnight, school districts around the country developed bullet-proof procedural protections — allowing (and sometimes providing) lawyers, preparing written transcripts, requiring third-party witnesses, even requiring separate student witnesses. Criminals probably wish they had some of the procedural protections of students. For teachers, exercising judgment as to the right thing to do was replaced by a preoccupation with how any decision might affect students' rights.

Disabled citizens had been largely ignored by law, probably because of society's tendency to want to forget about the misfortunes of those suffering from serious handicaps. Indignities were their daily routine: To someone in a wheelchair, every six-inch curb, every step, is like a high wall. The first toe in the water was a 1968 act that did not pass out general rights, but required that new or remodeled public buildings be wheel-chair-accessible. It was passed largely on the efforts of Hugh Gallagher, a wheelchair-bound aide to Senator E. L. Bartlett, of Alaska. The Rehabilitation Act of 1973, which funded disabled services, also resembled a traditional statute, except that soon before Congress voted on the bill, attorneys from the Office of Civil Rights of the Department of Health, Education, and Welfare (HEW) slipped in the following provision:

No otherwise qualified handicapped individual in the United States . . . shall solely by reason of his handicap, be excluded from participation in, be denied the benefits of, or be subjected to discrimination under any program or activities receiving federal financial assistance.

Known as Section 504, it quickly became a lightning rod. The language was absolute. What did it mean to "deny benefits" or "discriminate" in this context? Read literally, it meant that 16,000 school systems, 7,000 hospitals, 6,700 nursing homes and home health agencies, 2,600 institutions of higher learning, thousands of libraries, and every transit system had to be rebuilt to handicapped codes. The cost to New York City for modifying its subway system would alone be up

171

to $4 billion. The total cost nationwide was estimated by some to run over a hundred billion.

In passing the law, Congress did not acknowledge that even one dollar of cost was associated with this new right. When David Matthews, the secretary of HEW, asked for guidance, he was ignored. Congress was on to other things. Controversy over Section 504 raged for more than a decade, until it was finally amended to permit transit accommodations to be phased in over a number of years.

By that time, "504 Clubs" and other organizations of mainly wheelchair-bound citizens had formed to push for a broad application of the antidiscrimination mandate. In 1987, New York City passed a law that required wheelchair access not only to places of public accommodation but also to private apartments when newly built or remodeled. Any bathroom with a step up (as often occurs in new bathrooms in old buildings) would have to be eliminated or have a ramp; counters in kitchens would have to be adaptable to wheelchair level and to provide the space for a turning radius. Two-sided "Pullman" kitchens with narrow aisles, a typical configuration in a cramped city apartment, were essentially made illegal. The basic theory of these rights was that every housing unit should be wheelchair-friendly, just in case a wheelchair user wanted to live there. An architect, Richard Gould, observed that it would be cheaper by a few billion dollars to provide free housing to everyone in a wheelchair than to renovate 2 million apartments.

In 1990, using the rhetoric of the civil rights movement, and promising protection against discrimination to 43 million Americans, the now-potent lobby for the disabled succeeded in securing the Americans with Disabilities Act. The ADA gave the disabled the right to sue virtually every establishment, public or private, for discrimination. Minnetonka, Minnesota, had to alter the municipal hockey rink to make the scorer's box wheelchair-accessible. Under ADA regulations, doorknobs are now illegal in the workplace (they are hard to turn for someone without full use of his hands). So is carpet that is more than one quarter-inch thick (it causes too much friction for wheelchairs).

Retarded children, like the physically disabled, had also been ignored. When other children went to public school, their choice was to stay home or be locked in mental institutions. In 1972, a case brought by the Pennsylvania Association of Retarded Children secured a court order that retarded children, like all other children, were entitled to schooling. It did not prove hard to get legislative attention. As one observer noted, "The wretchedness of the treatment meted out . . . at institutions such as Willowbrook and Pennhurst and the specious nature of the rationale for excluding handicapped children from schools led reformers to demand radical change."

In 1975 Congress passed the Education for All Handicapped Children Act (now known as the

Individuals with Disabilities Education Act). The act gave disabled children rights to "specially designed instruction, at no cost to parents or guardians, to meet the unique needs of a handicapped child." Special procedures were also provided: Practically no decision could be made without the formal involvement of parents. Recalling Congress's preference in the 1850s for frontiersmen with "none of the education," bureaucrats were disqualified from making certain decisions if they had a "professional interest" in the issues that might interfere with their "objectivity."

Our confusion over government's role was complete: We wanted it to solve social ills, but distrusted it to do so. Congress had resolved this dilemma by using rights to transfer governmental powers to special interest groups.

The courts joined in, radically expanding the ability of citizens to sue. In a series of decisions in the late 1960s and early 1970s, the Supreme Court replaced the age-old requirement that a suing party have a "legal interest" (for example, a property owner affected by a new highway) with a right to sue government over practically any decision. Special interest groups, even those without new substantive rights, began to dominate policy through litigation.

Even animals got rights. The Endangered Species Act was passed, which made it unlawful to "take any such species." Almost immediately, the opponents of an almost-completed dam on the Tellico River in Tennessee found an indigenous

174

fish, the snail darter, whose habitat would be threatened if the river were turned into a lake. The Supreme Court, confronted with a right, felt it had no choice but to block the project. With all the money spent on the dam about to go down the drain, Congress passed a special law exempting the snail darter from the Endangered Species Act. The dam was built. The snail darter was able to overcome this treachery, and demonstrating its adaptability (an uncommon trait among special interest groups), it is doing swimmingly a few miles downstream.

Practically forgotten in the great rights rush is the original focus on racial integration. A few black leaders have noted how their crusade has become lost in a sea of rights. "The victims of the African slave trade," as Julian Bond has caustically observed, now find themselves pushed to the side by anyone who can register a complaint:

> Today the protected classes extend to a majority of all Americans, including white men over forty, short people, the chemically addicted, the left-handed, the obese, members of all religions. Surely there is a scholar somewhere who can tell us how we came to this state of affairs and how the road to civil rights became so crowded. . . . In our society, there were only so many fruits to go around. When short, fat, old white men step to the front of the line . . . then our

civil rights are as endangered as they were by Bull Connor and Sheriff Jim Clark twenty-five years ago.

Like printing money, handing out rights to special interest groups for thirty years has diminished not only the civil rights movement but the values on which it was founded. Rights, intended to bring an excluded group into society, have become the means of getting ahead of society. But everyone is losing. It is in the nature of continued conflict, as well as law's inadequacy as a vehicle to happiness, that the ostensible winners have found, not justice and fulfillment, but isolation and recrimination.

This is proving true even in the area where rights initially proved so effective, civil rights.

Like a Poison in the Air

Thirty years after passage of the Civil Rights Act, we should be witnessing a new age of cooperation and understanding in the workplace. Law has worked hard to do its part. Together in common endeavor, people should be getting to know each other as people. But has desegregation by law led to integration of the spirit, as Dr. King hoped? Is harmony around the corner? Do we have a new world of understanding between blacks and whites, women and men? Or are we, as some observers have noted, mired in

176

a deepening pit of isolation and mistrust?

Discrimination has become the preoccupation of our time. Even those who are successful are bitter. Ellis Cose, in *The Rage of a Privileged Class*, describes the extraordinary anger of successful blacks — partners in law firms, executives in companies — who feel they are being held back because of race: "I have done everything I was supposed to do. I have stayed out of trouble with the law, gone to the right schools, and worked myself nearly to death. *What more do they want?*" A black judge told me matter-of-factly that "everyone knows that a black professional has to do ten times as good a job to stay at the same place as a white."

These feelings mirror exactly, but in reverse, the feelings of white professionals who believe blacks are promoted primarily because they are black. To aspiring white male college professors, this issue touches a raw nerve, because limited teaching positions are now frequently reserved for minorities and women. According to one, "Everyone knows a friend who, after a decade of study, has been told not even to apply for the good jobs."

The civil rights movement was supposed to bring us together. Instead, it is as if we have climbed up the hill and, without noticing, have started sliding back down the other side. Reading through the contemporary political literature, whether by feminists, blacks, or conservative whites, one would have to conclude that repressed

177

ill will is turning the workplace into a powder keg.

And, increasingly, it is exploding. Discrimination claims are up 2,200 percent since 1969, the glory days when lawsuits were knocking down employment barriers right and left. Civil rights claims now account for 10 percent of the federal court civil caseload, proof that discrimination has, indeed, become an obsession. These are the so-called "good" claims, which can make it through the tollgate managed by the legal profession. According to Denny Chin, who until elevated to the federal bench specialized in representing discrimination claimants, the rule of thumb is that discrimination lawyers turn down nine out of ten employees who want to sue their former employers.

A paranoid silence has settled over the workplace. Only a fool says what he really believes. It is too easy to be misunderstood or to have your words taken out of context. You need not agree with Professor Richard Epstein, who would scrap antidiscrimination laws altogether, to recognize his fear of "[p]eople who are quick to impugn the motives and integrity of others, to find racial or sexual innuendo in innocent and everyday actions and speech." Most people are not that way, of course, but only one incident, or an anecdote about an incident, can chill an entire office. Employment lawyers generally tell their corporate clients to say as little as possible. According to one lawyer who has practiced in the field for twenty years, "You can't talk to anyone in a natural way." Manuals tell supervisors not to give evaluations without a script and a witness. Otherwise, he says, "it's too dangerous."

This is not just lawyer's caution. The country of the First Amendment no longer tolerates candor. Lawsuits spring out of the most routine events. There is a rash of litigation over "compelled self-defamation." Before you struggle too hard trying to figure out how people can defame themselves, here is the reasoning: It is because a negative job evaluation might have to be disclosed to a potential new employer. That at least has one cure: Tell all workers they're wonderful. But being too nice is also illegal: the Equal Employment Opportunity Commission is now investigating companies that give unduly rosy reviews of women and blacks. The theory, not illogical, is that false praise impedes self-improvement.

You may be in for a surprise if you want a new job and are relying on getting a good reference from a prior employer. References are quickly becoming a thing of the past. Employers rarely give them any longer, because there is a potential lawsuit in any message, whether a negative reference (which can be construed as an act of discrimination or defamation) or a glowing report ("So why didn't you promote me? It must be discrimination."). We might as well have our lips stitched up.

Without honest references, employers rely on word of mouth — friends of friends. It's too hard to know otherwise whether someone is any good. Even entry-level jobs work this way. One recent study examined why, in Brooklyn's Red Hook section, an area that includes both factories and public housing projects, the local residents couldn't get jobs. The issue was not race (most of the workers were black and Hispanic); nor did it turn out to be education. It was just that friends and families of existing workers were far more reliable than any people who lacked such connections. So nearby public housing residents, striving desperately to break their cycle of poverty and unemployment, couldn't get in the door.

Those hurt most by the clammed-up workplace are minorities and others whom the discrimination laws were intended to help. The dread of living under the cloud of discrimination sensitivity, and the real risk of litigation, often acts as an invisible door blocking any but the most ideal minority applicant. The head of a laboratory at a major university told me categorically that his department would not hire young black men because "we are afraid we can never get rid of them if they don't work out." Another university, after a nationwide search for a minority professor had narrowed the field to two candidates and it had hired one, then considered whether it should hire the second as well. It decided not to; the reasoning was that, "given that he is black, it will be impossible to deny him tenure."

The risk aversion seems greatest at smaller, entrepreneurial firms that don't relish having to bring in lawyers on ordinary personnel decisions. Who needs the headache? Minority employees thus seem to be funneled into boring jobs at large companies, fodder for mass-production white-collar work, but with no chance to show their special something.

Life within the workplace is also affected, and probably not as Dr. King had hoped. The absence of spontaneous give-and-take stifles the dream of mutual understanding, just as it diminishes enjoyment. Nor is it good for anyone's success. How can good ideas spring out, how can wrong turns be corrected, how can any aspect of business run effectively, if people are afraid to talk? The Rand Institute for Civil Justice has not measured the decline in interaction among employees, but it has measured other important effects of these laws; it found a decline in total employment by 2 to 7 percent in states with a higher incidence of discrimination and related lawsuits.

How did we get to be so sensitive? Why should an employer or coworker have anything to fear so long as he does not discriminate?

Think again about what discrimination is. It is evil motive: "You didn't promote me because of prejudice toward my race." How do you prove that? The law says there is nothing illegal about not liking someone's personality or about wanting to cut costs or, indeed, about being unfair — as long as it's not because of prejudice. How does a court know?

You may respond that the bigoted employer

is probably discriminating against others as well and that such a pattern — in one recent case, a supermarket chain that slotted all women into cashiers' jobs, without opportunity for promotion — would be powerful evidence. Judith Vladeck, one of the legal pioneers of the discrimination bar, said recently, "People who discriminate against a woman also generally discriminate against women." Indeed, the landmark class actions in the 1960s and 1970s proved precisely such patterns.

But class actions alleging a pattern of discrimination are virtually extinct. Now it is down to one-on-one. The twenty-two-fold increase in federal claims is mainly because of claims by individual workers who have been fired or laid off. Most of them do not even attempt to prove a pattern. Overt statements of hate or discrimination are also rare.

Prejudice obviously exists. But there is an unreliability, indeed an almost random quality, to one-on-one discrimination claims. Hitting someone or breaking a contract are matters easily measured by legal standards. Sexual harassment claims, although sometimes debated because of differences in view over social mores, nonetheless require abusive words or aggressive acts.

With one-person discrimination claims, often all there is, is the decision to fire or to not promote. Some people don't get along. There are widely differing views of performance and, even more, on intangibles like attitude. There is a big difference between what is good and what is adequate, between a helpful attitude and indifference, between double-checking and just doing the minimum. Some supervisors bring out the worst. There is, as we know, ample room for disagreement in the workplace.

How does a court sort through all this to find discrimination? If a case gets to trial, it usually boils down to a kind of popularity contest. The jury is asked to infer the employer's evil motive from a glowing presentation of the employee's competence and popularity. The employer defends itself by trying to show its own wisdom and the employee's weaknesses. Asides from some distant conversation often loom large. In one case a woman supervisor, who had been fired and replaced by a woman, nonetheless sued for sex discrimination. The main evidence? She had fired a man, and someone once called her a "treacherous bitch." "Lawyers take cases based on unfairness," says Denny Chin. "If there's not a good answer for the firing, they assume it's discrimination."

Stringing people up for an impure heart has provided some of the darkest moments in the history of law. Heresy trials in the Middle Ages often turned on politically incorrect statements, perhaps partially heard or misunderstood. The heresy trial of Jehan Orlhac in 1554, for example, focused on whether he had once said that "money given to priests did not profit a diseased soul." At the 1692 trial of Elizabeth Godman for witchcraft in Salem, Massachusetts, the main issue was whether she " 'cast a fierce look upon' a man, Stephen Goodyear, with the intention of causing him to fall into a 'swonding fitt.' "

Today's discrimination claims similarly lack an anchor of reliable fact. Most employers don't get rid of good workers. The person laid off is upset and angry and has every incentive to think the worst of the employer. Discrimination, particularly for blacks who suffer it daily at the hands of storekeepers and others in incidental encounters, is an easy conclusion. And all you have to allege is that the supervisor had a bad motive.

The White House was recently faced with a discrimination claim when an assistant chef, upon failing to be promoted, decided that this must have been because he married a black woman. Several years ago Glen-Gery Brick laid off several workers during a slow period, strictly on the basis of lack of seniority, and then was sued for discrimination by one of the workers, who had a disability. What does that do to Glen-Gery's incentive to hire disabled workers in the future?

The Kennedy School of Government has case studies on the use of discrimination charges as a form of extortion. In one study, a minority secretary refused to show up for months at a time at her government office, and when she did, she performed at best sporadically. She was warned repeatedly. At the end of the year, she demanded a promotion and sat in her supervisor's office, suggesting she would accuse him of racial bias if he did not write her a glowing recommendation. He did relent, according to the study, because he could not face the hearings and procedures required if she did make such a claim.

Discrimination has now become the common language of workplace disagreement. A new legal industry has arisen. Lose your job? Consult the Yellow Pages. The same lawyers who advertise for personal injury claims now seek out fired employees. It's just a business. Defending the claim can easily cost an employer more than $100,000, so there is a powerful inducement to settle. Even the most dedicated fighters of discrimination acknowledge, as one did to me, that "it is possible to create a discrimination claim out of almost any workplace dispute." The common law, by contrast, evolved with principles that tend to weed out claims that are unreliable or can be asserted too easily by those with an ax to grind.

The social benefit of this situation is hard to see. All around us, however, is the social wreckage. When law tries to reach its fist deep into our souls to wrench out lingering prejudices, it does so blindly. It bruises us right in our heart: "You are an evil bigot." The harm it inflicts, however, does not just occur with a claim. The damage begins well before any claim is brought. When almost any individual has been given the right to challenge someone else's motives, an essential condition for free interaction has been destroyed. The fear of a claim that can be based on an offhand comment or some other insignificant event is like a poison in the air.

To the rights-bearer, rights bring not the satisfaction of self-esteem but a quagmire of complicated feelings. Disappointment and bitterness are the inevitable products of a legal entitlement that promises a world free from prejudice but has no power to deliver it in ordinary human dealings. All you have to do is read Ellis Cose's book about successful blacks to see how the preoccupation with rights affects their lives. Black scholars debate the benefits, but few deny the costs. Racial preferences lead to "a kind of demoralization," as Professor Shelby Steele has put it, because "the quality that earns us preferential treatment is an implied inferiority."

The bitterness of the rights-bearer is immediately directed at other groups. "We express our concern for the oppressed or the victimized by hating the oppressor or the victimizer," James Q. Wilson has observed, and so we show our "anger at society" and "the ruling classes." Whites are the enemy. Men are the enemy.

Hate turns into a two-way street very quickly: How can we think about hate all the time without hating in return? Blacks are the enemy. Women are the enemy. Reverse-discrimination claims, generally brought by whites for undue preference to blacks, are one of the largest discrimination categories. With rights on the mind, every difference in perception can turn into resentment and feelings of injustice. Few more galling circumstances exist than a coworker who keeps his job despite perceived underperformance; in the poisoned atmosphere of "rights," people begin to assume it's special treatment.

The hate easily turns inward, particularly for those who, as Professor Steele terms, have assumed a "victim-focused identity." In Atlanta recently, a young black woman in government sued for discrimination because her supervisor, another black woman, allegedly resented her because she had a lighter complexion. The dispute was like a Ping-Pong match of descending discrimination charges: The testimony was that "dark-skinned blacks frequently suffered from color discrimination" by lighter-skin blacks, and thereby the supervisor, feeling discriminated against, discriminated back by telling her to "go get some sun." After the claim was filed, the supervisor was quoted as saying, "Why would she want to embarrass the black community this way? She's just a high-yella bitch." The preoccupation with purging prejudice is producing a nation filled with more prejudice.

Rather than smoothing the waters, Congress continues to agitate. In the Civil Rights Act of 1991, to assure "a discrimination-free workplace," Congress encouraged more lawsuits by stiffening penalties, allowing claims for emotional injury, and increasing attorneys' fees. The act's avowed purpose was "to encourage private citizens" to sue because "the principle of anti-discrimination is as important as the principle that prohibits assaults, batteries and other intentional injuries to people." Congress sees each employee as deputized to act as a "private attorney general to vindicate these precious rights. . . . It is in the interest of American society as a whole to assure that equality of opportunity in the workplace is not polluted by unlawful discrimination. Even the smallest victory advances that interest."

Congress has not noticed the practical impossibility of taking the crusade against prejudice down to each and every employee dispute. The House report quotes economist Heide Hartman for the proposition that "if discrimination costs money, people will stop doing it." But doing what? Giving candid reviews? Making personnel decisions using their best judgment? With "assaults, batteries and other intentional injuries," courts can easily find the evidence. No CAT scan has been invented to scrutinize our souls.

Our universities, it is often said, are a window to the future. If so, it is not a pretty vision. The obsession with the right to be free from discrimination has produced, on campuses across the nation, the scourge of political correctness. It would be a joke if anyone could figure out how to break out of it, but many who tried have regretted it. At Yale, a student who did a parody of "gay week" was almost thrown out of school. Nat Hentoff, in *Free Speech for Me but Not for Thee*, quotes the head of the Native American Students Association at Stanford, who, tired of being patronized, said, "When it reaches the point where sensitivity stifles communication, it has gone too far."

As Hentoff explains, enforced politeness hardly brings students together into a new world of understanding. Each group gravitates to its own kind, where they can at least say what they think. All-black dorms are now the norm. There are also Asian dorms and gay dorms. Dr. Irving Reid, the only black at Hamilton College in the class of 1953, returned in 1993 for his fortieth reunion and was approached by a black student who wanted to show him the "minority house." Dr. Reid declined: "I lived my life to prove that segregation was an irrational response to skin color. You now ask me to look with pride on your effort to segregate yourselves? How would you feel if someone forced blacks to all live together?"

Thirty years ago, with the Civil Rights Act of 1964, our country passed a landmark law that succeeded in breaking down many artificial barriers. The law did not eliminate prejudice, but it created an opportunity in which prejudice could begin to dissipate. Now, barely three decades later, we are well on our way to rebuilding those animosities. Discrimination is an open wound of our society, but, like animals, instead of caring for it as it heals slowly, we can't help but keep biting at it. The wound just opens up more.

The lesson should be clear: Law can only go so far. Dr. King tried to warn us:

Desegregation will break down the legal barriers and bring men together physically, but something must touch the hearts and souls of men so that they will come together spiritually because it is natural and right. . . . True integration will be achieved by true neighbors who are willingly obedient to unenforceable obligations.

Law must not promise to purge people's souls. It cannot. Law can set up the conditions for interaction and work toward changes over time. When it tries to do more, it only drives us further apart.

HAND OVER THE KEYS . . .

Do you think a disabled person should have the "right" to sit next to an airplane emergency exit? What if he takes an extra five minutes getting through the exit? Advocates for the disabled, who said that this only evened out the odds, lost this battle because of a conflicting statute of the Federal Aviation Administration. But they still insist their rights have been violated: To use their metaphor, they are being "forced to sit in the back of the bus."

At the time of the public-toilets controversy, a group of New York University professors pondered the ethical issues of valuing one group's desires over everyone else's. The problem they posed went like this: The extra cost of buses that have a lift for wheelchairs meant that 10 percent fewer buses were purchased; then service was cut back; then a grandmother in the Bronx had to wait an extra half hour in the cold in a dangerous neighborhood. Who, they wondered, was defending her rights?

Situations like this are not hypothetical. The mayor of Knoxville, Tennessee, announced that if the city had to divert millions of dollars for new "accessible" buses, it might have to curtail its bus service, used mainly by poor and elderly citizens. Because in part of wheelchair turning-radius requirements, each new subway train on New York City's No. 2 line will have 180 fewer seats available to ease the burden of tired feet.

Disabled citizens generally get what most would consider the front of the bus: Large cities provide door-to-door "paratransit" facilities for the disabled. But they also want to be "main-streamed." A friend from the neighborhood, Sara Medina, usually takes the bus up Third Avenue in Manhattan every morning, but now gets off and waits for another bus whenever the first one stops for a certain wheelchair user: "He takes almost ten minutes getting on and ten minutes getting off. I am late to work every time." How, indeed, should society balance six hundred lost minutes of thirty bus riders against the desire of one wheelchair user to take "mainstream" transportation instead of para-transit facilities that the city provides at no extra cost? According to

Sara Medina, "I feel guilty about it, but I can't help but be angry."

Making accommodations is critical. That's what government is supposed to do. Perhaps a city with a comprehensive bus system, like New York, should accommodate the disabled on regular buses while a city like Knoxville, whose bus system is marginal, should not. Maybe rush hour is the wrong time for mainstreaming. Choices have to be made, and the choice may well change from year to year. Instead, rights are handed out once and the legislature, basking in the praise of some group, has no clue about what the consequences will be.

In 1993, twenty-nine families in Southern California found themselves in the path of a raging fire. Temperatures from the fire reached 2000 degrees. There was no hope for their homes unless they quickly made fire-breaks by "discing" the ground around their homes with a tractor so the dried grass would be turned under. But their area is part of the habitat of the Stevens kangaroo rat, a protected species under the Endangered Species Act.

The fire showed no respect for the rats' rights and burned up both the rats and their habitat. As the fire bore down on the homes, it was pretty clear that saving the habitat wasn't in the cards. But no official had the power to make an exception to permit discing. A right to an undisturbed habitat, after all, is a right. The law said nothing about fires. Twenty-eight homes were incinerated. Michael Rowe, the owner of one home, went ahead and plowed his yard anyway: "How would it look if I got sent to Folsom or Sing Sing just because I saved my house?" The next week he found himself living in isolation on the charred landscape, a clapboard monument to the unwisdom of absolute mandates.

Public schools have been the hardest hit by the rights revolution. As a part of government, they get the brunt of every new interpretation of due process. The buildings are also public and so, as advocates of the disabled remind them in threatening letters and lawsuits, every light switch must be low enough to satisfy their rights. The greatest problem, however, and the source of such conflict that it seems headed for revolution, relates to the rights Congress gave to students for "special education."

Timothy W. was a profoundly disabled child. He was born with virtually no cerebral cortex and suffered severe brain damage from hemorrhaged hydrocephalus and meningitis. His other handicaps included cerebral palsy and cortical blindness, and he was quadriplegic. He could react to strong sensations like pain and certain smells, but he could do virtually nothing for himself except part his lips when being spoon-fed. He lived solely on his brain stem.

His mother, however, thought he should go to school. The local school district, in Rochester, New Hampshire, pulled together experts from around the Northeast and concluded that he was not "capable of benefiting" from educational services. Timothy's mother, showing a determination not uncommon in parents of disabled children, pressed her case. A federal appeals court eventually ruled that under the Individuals with Disabilities Education Act (known as IDEA), it didn't matter whether Timothy could benefit from education. The Rochester school district was obligated to provide an educational program. As one observer noted, under the court's decision, "school districts could be held responsible for children in comas."

The resolution of Timothy W.'s situation is not unique. Drew P., a multihandicapped child from rural Georgia, suffers from infantile autism and severe mental retardation. Although the state provided an extensive education program, including an expert in autism, Drew's parents were dissatisfied. They heard about a special school out of town. The school happened to be in Tokyo. A court ruled that the local school district had to foot the bill. In another case, the tab for a special education student was $200,000 per year. The law books are filling up with these cases as local school districts desperately try to stem the hemorrhaging of their budgets. But the school districts almost always lose. A right is a right.

The New York City Board of Education now spends 25 percent of its total budget on special education, covering about 10 percent of the students. It is a highly sophisticated program, but many parents demand more. One grandmother of a severely retarded girl from Brooklyn was not satisfied with any of the programs and couldn't be convinced, even by the head of special education for New York City. New York City now sends her granddaughter to a special school in Boston. "She wanted the very best," said the legal aid lawyer who represented her. "It will be great for seven years," says the lawyer, "and then she'll turn eighteen and be dumped back into the ghetto. It doesn't make a lot of sense."

How wonderful it would be if we could spend up to $200,000 annually on all girls and boys to maximize their potential. American public education, as we know, is not exactly on a roll. In a recent survey of education in twenty countries, our children barely avoided (courtesy of Portugal) coming in dead last in math. Many causes are cited, including two-worker families, television overdose, and lack of discipline. But one of the problems, according to one recent survey, is chronic underfunding. America spends less of its gross national product on education than any other major industrial country. But no other country spends more on education for the mentally disabled.

It is hard to fault parents who, naturally, do as much as possible for their disabled children. When measured against the statutory right for "specially-designed instruction . . . to meet the unique needs of each child," almost no level of support is enough. The blank check gets as many zeroes as parents can imagine.

But it's not just money. Congress also took away the authority of educators to make ordinary professional judgments. Special education teachers, who not many years ago considered themselves the "lone advocates for the handicapped child," now spend significant energies defending their judgments in administrative hearings. One federal judge found special education permeated with "an atmosphere of suspicion and mistrust," accompanied by "a decided emphasis on legal rights and entitlement at the forefront of the parents' approach." Parents constantly override the professionals, either by demanding a special school or by denying the problem altogether.

In one case in Chicago, the parents of a severely emotionally disturbed child, Adam P., refused to allow the school to transfer him to a special program in the school system for children with behavioral disorders. Instead, the parents insisted that Adam be "mainstreamed" in the regular junior high school. The result was that he was failing every course and, in the words of one teacher, "out of control." The parents nonetheless insisted that he was only learning-disabled, not behaviorally disturbed, and refused to permit the transfer. They also refused to allow the school to provide special social services. The case ended up being argued through the United States Court of Appeals where, given the clear rights of the act, the parents basically won.

In the figurative fistfight between professionals and parents, the child is generally the victim.

Mainstreaming is sometimes productive. But sometimes it is not, and it can imbue the disabled child with a sense of his inadequacies. Professor James Ysseldyck, of the University of Minnesota, who helped implement mainstreaming in Minneapolis schools, admitted that "it isn't working well . . . it's being used with good intentions but does some terrible things to kids." Pam Bloom, director of a special school for disabled children in New Jersey, refers to her students as "broken birds who have been ruined by the mainstreaming experience." Disabled high school students who spend time in regular classrooms have a failure rate of 61 percent; those in special education classes have a failure rate of 14 percent.

There are also, of course, all the other students to consider when a mentally disabled child is mainstreamed. Although each situation is different, significant disruption is common. The teacher's predicament is almost hopeless. Margaret Bays, a third grade teacher in Charleston, West Virginia, described what happened when a mainstreamed child would start making odd noises: "The whole class stops. . . . I feel I'm in a Ping-Pong game. The kids watch Aaron. Then they watch me. Then, while I'm busy with him, they act up."

A few years after passage of the act, the entire Minnesota congressional delegation described the effects in a letter to the Department of Education: "This law, whose good intentions we willingly grant, is surely one of the most badly drafted, mischievous acts ever inflicted on the children of Minnesota." How could it possibly work sensibly when it deprives professionals of their ability to make judgments? Whom do we trust more, professional educators or loving but zealous parents who go to bed every night longing for a miracle?

Congress, of course, never thought of most of this. It knew there was a lack of support for disabled children, so in the age of rights, it passed some out.

. . . AND WAIT TO GET RUN OVER

Handing out rights does not resolve conflict. It aggravates it. "Filing complaints is the keystone of the ADA," said one advocate for the disabled. To another, passage of the law is a call to "man the barricades." But against whom? The disabled lobby is waging warfare against every other citizen.

The fight for rights becomes obsessive, like a religious conviction. One former construction worker in Rhode Island, Gregory Solas, who has been in a wheelchair since an accident in 1986, has filed over two thousand complaints under disabled laws. He has single-handedly forced Rhode Island schools to spend millions of dollars to replace doorknobs with levers, to lower light switches and fire alarms, and to reconfigure showers. He once filed a claim when a father-daughter dance was held in a building that did not have a wheelchair ramp; the school was required to move the dance. Everyone else's enjoyment was of no moment compared to the price of being helped up a few steps. Mr. Solas is on a crusade, wielding his new rights like a sword while everyone else — the common good — is defenseless. Even the elected leaders of Rhode Island have no power.

Gifted students, in contrast to disabled children, receive virtually no support or attention from America's school systems; about two cents out of every hundred dollars is allocated to programs for them. According to a recent report by the U.S. Department of Education, gifted students languish in classrooms bored stiff, doing their work left-handed, having mastered over half the curriculum before the school year begins. Nothing is done to nurture their skills or groom them to be future leaders of education, business, or government.

The ratio of funding of special education programs to gifted programs is about eleven dollars to one cent. I doubt that many legislators or officials think this balance makes sense. But Congress took away everyone's power to balance the competing needs. As columnist Anna Quindlen has observed, it's "Just dumb": We have built an educational system "obsessed with its potential failures to the detriment of its potential successes."

The virtue of rights, at least to the advocates,

is that they are absolute. What's a little inefficiency when there is complete justice for me? Absolutes sound good, but generally leave behind a landscape of paradoxes and bruised victims.

Rights for the disabled are particularly paradoxical, because what benefits a person with one disability may harm someone with another disability. Low drinking fountains and telephones are harder to use for the elderly or those with bad backs. High toilets make transfer easier from a wheelchair, but make bowel movements harder for everyone else, especially the elderly. Curb cuts are more dangerous for the blind, who have more difficulty knowing when they have reached the end of the block. Ramps are essential for wheelchairs but are sometimes slippery and dangerous for the frail. Warning bumps at the edge of a train platform are good for the blind but bad for those in wheelchairs. When confronted by a dwarf complaining that certain of the changes for the disabled made his life miserable, the director of New York's Office for the Disabled is reported to have said, "You can't please everybody." Exactly. So why is it appropriate to handle these issues as a "right"?

Rights are a kind of wealth and, like other forms of wealth, attract hangers-on. Anyone who wants something looks around to see if it fits within the orbit of some right. In recent years the number of disabled children has grown, not very mysteriously, as parents have learned that characterizing a problem as a "learning disability" carries with it special treatment. Soon, as with the proliferation of categories of citizens protected against discrimination, perhaps a majority of children will lay claim to a disability. Gifted children could claim boredom as their own special handicap.

The Endangered Species Act has attracted the antidevelopment forces. There are consultants who, for $10,000 or so, will try to find some indigenous minnow or mouse that can be used to block a proposed development. There are, after all, an estimated 30 million species of animals in our country, most of which are not even known.

The northern spotted owl of the Pacific Northwest forests turns out to be the exact same species, *Strix occidentalis,* that thrives in habitats a little further south, from California down to Mexico. The difference is that climate makes coloring of feathers slightly different, depending where in the north-south range it lives. Some people undoubtedly cared about preserving the owl's place in this northern habitat, even though the owl could find plenty of friends a few miles south. But a lot of people cared about the ancient Northwest forest that loggers wanted to start chopping down. The forest did not have rights; the spotted owl did. So a debate about cutting forests was turned into a war over the rights of the "northern" spotted owl. The ultimate resolution — taxpayers spending $1.3 billion to retrain loggers who no longer had trees to cut — was revealing both of the purpose of the crusade and the power of rights.

The Americans with Disabilities Act supposedly protects 43 million Americans. The overwhelming preponderance of the ADA regulations, however, and virtually all cost and conflict, relate to wheelchair users. But there are not 43 million people in wheelchairs. There are not 10 percent of that number of people in wheelchairs. It turns out, in a number that seems to have been actively suppressed (I could find it nowhere in the extensive legislative history), that not 2 percent of the disabled are in wheelchairs, and many of those are confined to nursing homes. Billions are being spent to make every nook and cranny of every facility in America wheelchair-accessible (for example, by tearing down and rebuilding showers), when children die of malnutrition and finish almost dead last in math.

Zealots, we learn time and again, always push their "right" to its absolute limit and beyond. They go as fast as they can, the rest of us be damned. "The law is the law," Mr. Solas says: "If I could, I would make them stand at a chalkboard and write, 'I will not discriminate.' " Their mission becomes an obsession, their appetite never quelled. Faster and faster. It's their right.

But we all live here together. Society needs red lights as well as green lights. Government — whether Congress or local school boards — must continually perform the role of letting one group go so far and then allowing others to go.

Rights provide a perpetual green light. That means everyone else is getting run over as those with rights try to get to where they want.

The injuries are mounting, and Americans are building up a reservoir of hatred. Just listen to radio talk shows.

Society can be as liberal as we want it to be. But that requires a mechanism, which democracy used to try to provide, for injecting common sense and working out compromises. I would favor, for example, significant funding for wheelchair access. But I would also have an easy mechanism for waivers: The hockey scorer's box in Minnetonka can manage without it. I would probably also support money to save the ancient Northwest forest, but maybe not $1.3 billion. I would certainly want to provide decent and loving care for disabled children, including those who are unlikely ever to be productive members of society. But I would not send them to Tokyo.

BINDING THE FEET
OF THE WELFARE STATE

In the night of November 29, 1993, Yetta Adams froze to death while sitting erect on a bus stop bench in front of the Department of Housing and Urban Development (HUD) in Washington, D.C. She was, by the accounts of those who knew her, a gentle person whose troubles included addiction to painkillers and clinical depression. Her tragedy is not uncommon — an unidentified man was found frozen to death next to the Library of Congress a few days later — but the place where she died, perhaps where she chose to die, put the story on national news. HUD secretary Henry Cisneros, speaking at her funeral at Carron Baptist Church, said that "something is not right," and pledged $250,000 for more temporary beds in Washington. Rev. Lester W. Allen, in his eulogy, said: "I'm convinced that those in positions of authority are sincere . . . but you don't mind if I tell you truth now, do you? . . . Beloved, they have never solved our problems."

To social reformers, caring for people in need and respecting their rights are almost the same thing. The rights revolution, after all, sprouted from the same ideological seed as the Great Society. If providing care means giving out a welfare check, having the right to get it is, indeed, about the same thing. But helping people like Yetta Adams is not a matter of legal entitlements but a complicated human dilemma. Ministers like Rev. Allen or my father, whose ministry included one of the poorest areas of Appalachia, know that better than most. It requires genuine caring and good sense. Passion and conflict are not unusual. No person, no day with that person, is the same. Progress doesn't come out of formulas, and certainly not legal forms.

Charles Reich, pushing his "new bill of rights for the disinherited," believed that people needed independence, not help. The very idea of helping raised hackles. He focused on the abuses of over-bearing paternalism, and particularly the idea that social workers would have any measure of discretion over welfare benefits. Legal rights, by providing freedom and dignity, would permit people to pull themselves out of the pit of dependence. He had a point, and, sensing a new age of rights, the Supreme Court turned theory into law: Government would not be able to do anything except by observing due process.

Making a reasonable judgment was no longer sufficient. The judgment must be made in the right way: Did the welfare recipient or the suspended student have the opportunity to clearly present his side of the case? Due process also implies an obligation of uniformity, which means anyone can sue if he thinks he's not being treated the same as others. Most significantly, due process implies private ownership in the government's decision, keeping government on the defensive even when it is providing services. Going by the book, not making their best judgment, became the only safe path for providers in the welfare state. After all, failing to satisfy any one of the requirements of this due process could get you sued. To Reich, redefining government services as a "new property" protected by the Constitution accomplished the desired independence from the state.

It worked brilliantly. The social welfare system, which once considered its assignment to be hands-on, now considers the job to be hands-off. The welfare "caseworkers" that Reich so loathed basically no longer exist. They have become clerks whose job it is not to understand and deal with human problems but to make sure that all the legal regularities are followed. When I asked a former general counsel of New York City's welfare department to describe its social services, he didn't initially even comprehend the question. "Our agency doesn't provide social services," he said. "Its function is management of entitlements."

Due process does not, unfortunately, put more bread on the table; government can set benefits at whatever level it wants. What due process puts on the table is a thick manual of rules designed to ensure uniformity and procedural regularity. Paternalism is replaced with bloodless formalism. People in need get lots of law.

It is difficult to imagine a system that more perfectly combines the evils of inhumanity and ineffectiveness. All you have to do is visit a welfare office to believe that it was designed by a demon. It is a world where the recipient is barely known to the clerk. The "face-to-face" meetings required every six months are a form of torture: A forgotten Social Security card or other required piece of documentation leads to termination of benefits. Waiting for the interrogation under fluorescent lights is itself part of the torture: One documentary showed several elderly people sitting in the waiting area all day, the main movement being the hands of the clock. The end of the day came around, and it showed them being asked to leave. You keep asking yourself, What did they need? Were they hungry?

Compassion is nonexistent, because compassion is basically unlawful. Why should one person get special help? Who is to decide? The specter of favoritism drives the social reformer back to the volume of rules. All must be the same. Rights, as Professor Joel Handler has noted, only get in the way of a "cooperative, continuing relationship. . . . The situation calls for a community. . . . Instead of sensitive, individualized exploration of needs, nonfinancial as well, there is mindless application of harsh rules, people treated as objects, and a proletarianized staff. The program of rights has turned into a cruel hoax. It is bureaucratic rationality at its worst."

Several years ago, to prevent eviction of families who had fallen behind on paying rent for reasons beyond their control, New York City decided to set aside a fund to advance rent payments for those in need. The advances would be discretionary; otherwise, lines of people would stretch around the corner and soon the funds would be exhausted. The program hinged in part on the judgment of individual welfare officials: Is the applicant generally responsible, or does he habitually divert rent money to drugs or alcohol? Does his explanation make sense? But legal aid lawyers, representing clients who were turned down, sued on the basis that everyone wasn't treated the same. The upshot was a fixed rule that, because of limited funds, excludes relief to many deserving families.

Observing the forms of due process, and wrapping every decision in layers of defensive legal justifications, makes the scene tidy and safe to a remote overseer at a prestigious law school or on the bench of the Supreme Court. Like those who bound the feet of Chinese women, they take aesthetic pleasure in watching the welfare state shuffle along safely in accord with rigid legal conventions. Who can criticize them, the shapers of law, for a system that shows legal respect and ensures sameness?

Imposing due process, however, is inconsistent with helping human beings. Abiding by its formalisms, and satisfying uniformity, carves a chasm between helper and helpee. The welfare state is reduced to throwing crumbs from a distance because of a tragic misfit of legal ideology and social objectives.

Having its traditional authority depleted also made it difficult for government to manage the provision of services, whether allocating resources or controlling misbehavior. People with a talent for manipulation soon filled the void, to the injury of everyone else. This is illustrated well by the simplest and least controversial social service: public education.

Until the Supreme Court held that education had to be treated as a "property right," no one ever thought that due process had anything to do with running an elementary school or deciding to suspend an unruly eleventh grader. Principals and teachers had the authority to make decisions. Students, and their parents, did not think of their "rights." They had none. If you didn't do your homework, you flunked. If you misbehaved, you were suspended or put on probation. Most experts still believe that authority is important in dealing with children and adolescents.

Due process in schools came up in the atypical context of political demonstrations. The Supreme Court did not intend to turn discipline upside down. But as Justice Lewis Powell warned in a dissenting opinion, more was at stake than a nice theory that some law professors had dreamed up:

> The State's interest . . . is in the proper functioning of its public school system for the benefit of *all* pupils and the public generally. Few rulings would interfere more extensively in the daily functioning of schools than subjecting routine discipline to the formalities and judicial oversight of due process.

According to a nationwide survey of teachers by Catherine Collins and Douglas Frantz, there is now "an atmosphere of terror" in many urban schools. But the greater harm is not violence, according to Albert Shanker, president of the American Federation of Teachers, but the disruption of learning caused by the breakdown of order: "[D]isruption is far more common than violence in our schools, and it's routinely destructive to learning. All you need is one kid who sits in the back of the room shouting put-downs at other students to guarantee that very little learning takes place."

Due process deprived teachers and principals of the authority to respond to difficult situations immediately. According to George Jacobs, principal of Sandberg Junior High School in suburban Chicago, "Twenty or thirty years ago kids who habitually misbehaved were easy to distinguish and we could do something about it immediately. Today I have to build a record." Except in the cases of the most egregious student conduct, most teachers often don't bother to act at all: The procedures they have to follow are just too onerous. One result is that bad kids, realizing that teachers have their hands tied, play it to the hilt.

One observer tells of interviewing a teacher in Boston who "was still shaking as she told about a group of students who had verbally assaulted her and made sexually degrading comments about her in the hall." She said she didn't report the incident, however, because "it wouldn't have done any good." The reason? "I didn't have any witnesses." Thirty years ago, as another observer has noted, an assault like this on a teacher would have been dealt with so swiftly that it would have been unthinkable.

Nancy Udell, a former teacher and dean at Walton High School in the Bronx, tells the story of a disruptive student who assaulted a security guard in an incident witnessed by another officer, a teacher, and a dean. The student's suspension was rejected, however, because in New York, as in many cities, student witnesses are required for any significant discipline. George Jacobs from Sandberg Junior High recalls one incident in which he finally dropped the suspension of a student for selling drugs after the parents pressed it to the third level of the appeals process: "I refused to continue calling student witnesses. I decided that requiring them to participate in this hostile and cynical process was more detrimental than any benefit that might have been received by fair discipline. . . . By the way," Jacobs noted, "that student was eventually kicked out of high school for drug dealing."

The tragedy, according to Nancy Udell, is that the troublemakers are comparatively few in number: "Everybody thinks that all the kids are bad at large inner city high schools. It's not true. But the few who are ruin it for everyone else." Ms. Udell estimated that there were fifty real troublemakers out of three thousand students at Walton: "If we could have gotten rid of those fifty, it would have been a completely different school."

The situation is also taking its toll on the teachers. One psychiatrist, after evaluating 575 teachers, concluded that their "extraordinary and continuing stress bore a striking resemblance to combat neurosis among the psychiatric casualties of World War II." In the Collins and Frantz survey, many teachers expressed their frustration at not being able to do their job: "Society is a terrible place now because children have so many rights"; "When they gave kids rights and parents rights, it meant hands-off"; "Discipline [is] . . . the number one issue"; "What you need in the public schools first, is the ability to kick kids out."

To those managing the welfare state, the rights revolution offered one enormous benefit: Rights provide the perfect excuse for inaction.

Homelessness is perhaps the starkest symbol of the failure of a rights-based social welfare system. Indeed, the failure is so perfect that we almost take homelessness for granted. But it was only around 1980 that we began to notice people living on the streets. They displayed a different pattern from the alcoholics on skid row. Wrapped in layers of clothing, caked with dirt, they would sometimes stare, sometimes beg, sometimes scream. But we refused to act on the obvious, that most of them were mentally incapacitated or debilitated by drugs. In an age of rights, we kept our distance. Who were we to interfere with their lives? Arguments over what to do centered on their rights, not their realities.

Advocates for their welfare gave them a name, the "homeless," and promoted the idea that they had a legal right to a home, that a selfish society had let ordinary people slip through the safety net onto the streets. In the first bloom of advocacy for the homeless, Joyce Brown, a homeless woman who renamed herself Billie Boggs after a local newscaster, was taken up to

Harvard where, according to reports, she delivered a passable lecture: "I was a political prisoner. I did not commit a crime. My problem was that I did not have a place to live." Then she returned to New York, basking in the national spotlight and all the attention government could provide. A temporary residence was found. She got a job typing for the American Civil Liberties Union.

Mrs. Jacqueline Williams, a mother of fourteen children in Washington, D.C., appeared on *Donahue* describing the horror of life at the bottom of the social welfare state. Shuttling her large family from shelter to shelter evoked images of fleeing refugees and embarrassed the city into finding her a large house and making sure that public assistance was available. Billie Boggs and Jacqueline Williams were the models of how a humane government could deal with the phenomenon of homelessness.

Within three weeks Billie Boggs, having gone off her medicine, was back on the street, "swearing . . . and screaming." Within one year Jacqueline Williams had to be moved out of the house. It was a wreck: "Plumbing fixtures had been ripped out and the house was filled with trash, debris and human waste." The reality was that both women were sick; neither could take care of herself and neither could function without active intervention.

We are rightly cautious whenever interfering with someone's freedom. But mental illness is a fact that cannot be wished away. Commitment to a mental institution has always required judicial approval in our country. On the other hand, it is all too easy to then forget about the patient. When neglect and indifference in mental institutions were exposed in the 1960s, there was an irresistible fit with the rights revolution. Movies like *One Flew Over the Cuckoo's Nest*, based on Ken Kesey's novel, promoted the view of radical reformers that mental illness was only society's tag for people with a different point of view. In the words of one reformer, Thomas Szasz: "If there is no psychiatry, there can be no schizophrenics. . . . Hence, if psychiatry is abolished, schizophrenics disappear."

Advocates went to court and succeeded in limiting involuntary commitment unless the person was shown to be "dangerous to himself or to others." Willowbrook and other institutions opened their gates, and thousands of mentally ill patients not thought to be dangerous came into society. Most experts agree that "deinstitutionalization" is a good idea, as long as there is outpatient care on the outside. States proved very effective at closing down the mental institutions, which were a huge budgetary drain. They soon forgot their promises about community care facilities.

A "right to refuse treatment" was the next shoe to drop. The problem, as one observer has noted, is the idea of will: "The Catch-22 is that the diseased organ is the brain. . . . [A] very high proportion of the mentally ill do not recognize there is anything wrong with them."

For years, these new rights had little noticeable impact. The patients who were "deinstitution-alized" were accustomed to treatment, and found family and others willing to provide needed attention. Most of the homeless mentally ill on the streets today, however, became sick in an era when institutions were not generally available to them. Most never knew the treatment a mental institution can provide, and many refuse treatment.

The effects are tragic. One distraught mother said this of rights for the mentally ill: "The authorities say it is our son's choice and right to live like a stray animal. Why is rapid suicide illegal and gradual suicide a right?" The American Psychiatric Association, in a task force report, said that rights for the homeless "cloak neglect in the banner of freedom."

Government acts like a weak volunteer, as if it is not qualified to question the right of psychotics to choose to remain psychotic. But who else do we have to make these judgments? Are we really so close to authoritarianism that we can't help those who are sick? Do we think doctors are going to start performing random lobotomies or doping people for their political views? Is it that hard to devise a reasonable method of judicial oversight?

The responsibility to manage the lives of the homeless falls, by default, to the police — who pick them up on cold days or when they are disrupting a neighborhood and then do it again with the same person the next week. Jails and shelters have replaced mental institutions. One survey in the mid-1980s found 26,000 mentally ill people in prison. Shouldn't the police be dealing with crime instead of acting as ward attendants in an outdoor mental institution? Are cold doorways and jail cells more humane than hospitals?

"Thirty years ago Yetta Adams never would have frozen to death," said Roger Conner, the head of the American Alliance of Rights and Responsibilities. "We understood then that some people need intervention, not legal rules protecting them from intervention."

Yetta Adams lived most of her adult life with the benefits of due process rights granted in *Goldberg* v. *Kelly*. Her situation cried out not for protection from social workers but for a close relationship with one. For years, her life was a revolving door in and out of mental institutions and shelters. She finally moved in with a grown son, but he went to jail for robbing a McDonald's. The week before she died she checked out of a shelter without a word. When found on the bench across from the HUD building, she had three hundred dollars on her, more than enough to come out of the cold. But she chose not to.

To reformers in the 1960s, rights seemed logical as a framework for defining relations with the welfare state. After all, the Bill of Rights stakes out the boundaries between individuals and government. But the Bill of Rights did not ask government to provide services; it told government to stay away. When we demand that the welfare state address difficult human problems like poverty and homelessness, and ordinary ones like education, we must allow the humans doing the job to operate appropriately. We need all the resources, including compassion, that they can bring to bear on those tasks. We want to encourage them to take responsibility, not bind them up in formalistic and defensive procedures as if we were trying to *prevent* them from doing their jobs.

We have accepted the pretense that government services should be treated as a constitutional right. They are not; they are only benefits provided by a democracy. Nor is our choice limited to either constitutional rights or authoritarianism. Teachers can have obligations not to be arbitrary without giving a selfish adolescent a constitutional right to disrupt the entire class. Social workers can be held accountable for inappropriate behavior without making them comply with endless procedures. Why not just let them do their jobs?

Not in memory, as Rev. Lester W. Allen suggested at Yetta Adams's funeral, has the welfare state helped solve any of our hard problems. In fairness, it has barely tried.

CONFUSING POWER WITH FREEDOM

Handing out rights was supposed to provide justice in a fragmented society. But social structure cannot be divided up like land: We all live here together. Rights have ended up dividing society with deep legal fissures that zig and zag across the landscape of special interests.

Any legal device so disruptive must suffer from deeper infirmities. And so it is with the modern rights we invented in the last few decades. Looking back to basic principles, we know that many Americans died to protect the rights that our founders gave us. These rights, as we were told time and time again in school, are the foundation of a free society. But what does that mean? The platitude is so worn that it slides off the brain without imparting understanding.

It may be helpful to restate it this way: The rights that are the foundation of this country are rights *against* law. In James Madison's words, the Constitution provides for "protection of individual rights against all government encroachments, particularly by the legislature." Rights — freedom of speech, property rights, freedom of association — were to be the antidote against any new law that impinged on those freedoms.

The Constitution nowhere prohibits Congress from handing out new rights, however, as long as basic freedoms are not interfered with. Because the causes that the new rights support are invariably worthy, why not support these special interests as much as possible?

Curbing power in the hands of special interests, however, was another important goal of the republic. These special interests were referred to as "factions" that, described by James Madison in *Federalist 10*, should be familiar to modern Americans:

> By a faction, I understand a number of citizens who are united and actuated by some common impulse of passion, or of interest, adverse to the rights of the other citizens, or to the permanent and aggregate interests of the community.

Madison understood that factions are "sown in the nature of man," stemming inevitably from differences of wealth and circumstances. The goal of the republic was to create a system that would "emphasize deliberation" by government rather than allowing the passion or power of a particular cause to take hold.

Legislating open-ended rights is the opposite of "emphasizing deliberation." With rights, a special interest group can define the scope of its new power through the courts, not through elected representatives. Creating rights also invites a free-for-all as different groups' entitlements begin to collide with each other and the rest of society.

This conflict is the inevitable consequence, as the philosopher Isaiah Berlin explained, of the right "to" anything. The right to universal health care, for example, is currently at the top of the national agenda. Medical decisions, however, are hard enough — say, on whether to spend millions on premature and brain-damaged newborns — without having to deal with the problem as a "right." What happens when the money runs out and there is none left for victims of breast cancer or heart attack?

The injury is deeper than fights over money. Citizens feel an almost involuntary resentment when they see that other citizens, directly or indirectly, are ordering them around. Whether it is a group of liberal New York University professors who are offended by advocates for the disabled blocking a test of public toilets, or the repressed anger of a worker who feels that the person at the next station is being held to a different standard, or the frustration of teachers who are prevented from doing the right thing, the effect is to splinter society.

Why should this be? Rights sound so righteous. But the new rights aren't rights at all: They are blunt powers masquerading under the name of rights. They have nothing to do with rights. The rights our forefathers died for are a shield — government can't tell me what to do or say — to preserve our freedom from others ordering us around. The new rights are a sword. They are hailed under the flag of freedom. But no one doing the saluting is looking at how these rights impinge on what others consider to be their own freedoms. The coinage of the new rights regime has a flip side; it is called coercion.

There may be rare occasions when rights could be the appropriate vehicle for change, as they were in the civil rights movement. The inevitable conflict that erupts may sometimes be worth it, as it was in the South in the 1960s. But is that heroic crusade, whose wounds have not yet healed, the one we want to emulate in the daily decisions of democracy?

Rights are not, as Charles Reich hoped, an instant method for reform. They are the perfect formula for tearing society apart. The right to life is unassailable. So is the right to freedom of choice. Where does that leave us? In a civil war. We have forgotten to consult our operating manuals. Madison wrote in *Federalist 51* that "in forming a government of men over men, the greatest difficulty lies in this: . . . You must enable government to control the governed; and in the next place oblige it to control itself." When it hands out rights, government does the opposite: It abdicates its prerogatives and loses its ability to control the governed.

Rights are not the language of democracy. Compromise is what democracy is about. Rights are the language of freedom, and are absolute because their role is to protect our liberty. By using the absolute power of freedom to accomplish reforms of democracy, we have undermined democracy and diminished our freedom.

IV

RELEASING
OURSELVES

A mericans can do almost anything. We'll figure it out, and if we don't, we'll work so
hard it won't matter. Our energy has always
amazed foreigners. As Tocqueville observed:

> No sooner do you set foot on American
> soil than you find yourself in a sort of tumult;
> a confused clamor rises on every side and
> a thousand voices are heard at once. . . .
> All around you, everything is on the move.

The atmosphere, however, has changed.
"Americans feel on a daily basis that their society
is falling apart, that things aren't working right,"
says Michael Lerner, the editor of *Tikkun* mag-
azine. A sense of "collective powerlessness," as
political scientist Stanley Renshon puts it, is now
pervasive. The fresh air of self-determination has
been replaced, according to Professor Cornel
West, by "self-paralyzing pessimism."

But Americans haven't changed. Whenever the
rules are eased, our energy and good sense pour
in like sunlight through opened blinds. After the
1994 earthquake in Los Angeles toppled freeways,
California governor Pete Wilson suspended the

thick book of procedural guidelines and, using federal aid, authorized financial incentives for speedy work. Instead of a four-year trudge through government process, the Santa Monica freeway was rebuilt in sixty-six days, to a higher standard than the old one.

From law's perspective, the Los Angeles repair project was a nightmare of potential abuse. The process wasn't completely objective; almost nothing was spelled out to the last detail. When the rule book got tossed, all that was left was responsibility. State officials took responsibility for deciding which contractors would be allowed to bid, and they knew they would be accountable if the contractors proved unreliable. Instead of specifying every iron rod, state inspectors took responsibility for checking to make sure that the work complied with general standards. When disagreements occurred, the contractor and the state bureaucrats worked them out, just as if they were real people. And they got it done in record time.

"When they see how we do on this one," laughed Dwayne Robertson, an ironworker on the Santa Monica freeway, "they're going to want them all completed this fast." "I feel proud," said Necie Mitchell, a pile driver. "It feels good knowing you had a stake in rebuilding L.A."

BANISHING THINKING

Like tired debaters who say the same thing over and over, our political parties argue relentlessly over government's goals, as if our only choice is between big brother or the laissez-faire state. They agree on little, but are in complete accord on this: Law is black or white, or it is not law. Once their debate ends and the vote is taken, they put every detail and procedure into the legal machine and leave it in the care of bureaucratic technicians. There is no need for them, or us, to think about it anymore. It's the law now.

They miss the problem entirely. Our hatred of government is not caused mainly by government's goals, whatever their wisdom, but by government's techniques. How law works, not what it aims to do, is what is driving us crazy.

Freedom depends at least as much on deciding how to do things as on deciding what to do. Thousands of rigid rules are not needed to satisfy the important goal of worker safety; people could come up with their own plan, as Glen-Gery Brick did, and do a much better job. Our "primary concern," Professor Larry Preston has suggested, "should be to create arrangements that support our freedom to choose."

Law is hailed as the instrument of freedom because without law, there would be anarchy, and we would eventually come under the thumb of whoever gets power. Too much law, we are learn-

227

ing, can have a comparable effect: Millions of tiny legal cubicles give humans virtually no leeway. Unlike any legal system we ever admired, it tells us what to do and exactly how to do it.

It is no coincidence that Americans feel disconnected from government: The rigid rules shut out our point of view. Americans feel powerless because we are not given a choice: Modern law does not allow us, to quote Justice Cardozo, "to complete and correct the rigidity of instruction by the suppleness of instinct."

In a system of final rules, every decision is a binary choice. Yes or no, legal or illegal, proper procedure or Return to Go, we are constantly poked by legal dictates that keep us in our predetermined place. "The rule of joy and the law of duty," Holmes once observed, "seem to me all one." Today, we have lost our joy, and much more, because modern law tells us our duty is only to comply, not to accomplish. Understanding of the situation has been replaced by legal absolutism.

Government approaches its new tasks every year in the same absolutist way: Problems must be solved once and for all. With enough procedures, no bureaucrat will ever again put his hand in the till; and so, as uncovered in 1994, the Defense Department spends more on procedures for travel reimbursement ($2.2 billion) than on travel ($2 billion). No humiliation will ever again confront a wheelchair-bound citizen; and so we squander billions rebuilding places where few, if any, inconveniences would ever occur. Progress, it seems too obvious to point out, requires balancing all of society's goals, not treating each as an obsession.

When humans are not allowed to make sense of the situation, almost nothing works properly. In their 1982 critique of regulatory methods, *Going by the Book*, Eugene Bardach and Robert Kagan quoted a nursing home inspector who, when asked to state "the single most important variable in making a nursing home into a decent place," replied without hesitation, " 'The charge nurse. If she is competent and *cares* about her job, the place will be alright; otherwise, forget it.' " In reaction to rigid federal laws passed after the S&L crisis, Derrick Cephas, New York's superintendent of banks, made a similar point: "Not every banking problem can be resolved by the enactment of a rule or regulation. . . . Good banking regulation, just like good banking itself, requires experience and judgment."

By exiling human judgment in the last few decades, modern law changed its role from useful tool to brainless tyrant. This legal regime will never be up to the job, any more than the Soviet system of central planning was, because it can't think. The comedy of law's sterile logic — large POISON signs warning against common sand, spending twenty-two years on pesticide review and deciding next to nothing, allowing fifty-year-old white men to sue for discrimination — is all too reminiscent of the jokes we used to hear about life in the Eastern bloc.

Judgment is to law as water is to crops. It should not be surprising that law has become brittle, and society along with it. Any sensible system of law, as legal philosopher H.L.A. Hart observed, must offer its citizens "a fresh choice between open alternatives."

LAW THAT ALLOWS THINKING

None of us has difficulty understanding the goals of a safe workplace, a pleasant nursing home, or a clean meat-packing plant. Room for dispute always exists but, measured by accepted norms, only within a certain range. Sir Frederick Pollock, professor of jurisprudence at Oxford and friend of Holmes, once observed that there is "more of honest truth in the inspiring generality" than in "many an arid" rule.

Before American law became the world's thickest instruction manual, it worked on general principles that reflected the law's goals. The common law has plenty of rules and guidelines, but they are subservient to broader principles. If applying a guideline in a particular case seems inconsistent with the principle, an exception is made. "Rules dictate results, come what may," the legal philosopher Ronald Dworkin noted. "Principles do not work that way; they incline a decision one way, though not conclusively," and permit a judgment that fits the situation. Principles allow us to think.

Regulating isn't nearly as hard as we've made it. Getting rid of the obsession with preordained rules allows us to acknowledge, for example, that every factory has a different environmental profile. Complying with a nearly endless checklist of legal requirements, most not relevant to any given factory, simply bogs everyone down in hip-deep law. Meanwhile, at the nozzle nobody looked at, the benzene wafts free. As Randall Browning, an Amoco environmental manager, put it: "What is the point of spending $31 million to solve a problem that wasn't a problem while doing nothing about the real problem? What we are looking for is a new approach. Give us a goal to meet rather than all the regulations." Issues like the environment are too complicated to control rigidly out of an instruction manual, and the attempt has created a hopeless legal tangle.

Britain's Inspectorate of Pollution, considered highly effective, works in the opposite way. It enforces pollution control against a legal principle to reduce pollution "by the best means practicable." Its "relationship to the manufacturer is more like that of a doctor getting the patient's cooperation in treating a disease than that of a policeman apprehending a culprit." Britain has "presumptive standards," but they are not binding on anybody who has a better idea or can show a special problem. There are almost no absolutes.

Discarding the idea of universal requirements permits the picture of each polluter to become clear immediately. To use the words of philosopher Michael Oakeschott, we "can get the square meal of experience." Former environmental commissioner Tom Jorling discovered that in New York State 95 percent of stationary pollution (everything except cars and trucks) comes from four hundred plants. Four hundred plants is a drop in the bucket compared with the four thousand New York State environmental employees who, year after year, spend all their time trying to shuffle forms and untangle the rules. In the country as a whole, Jorling estimates that fewer than five thousand plants generate virtually all of the stationary pollution. Because each factory has a polluting personality that is different, Jorling suggests, why not customize regulation for each factory? Remember again how obvious the solution was when EPA and Amoco stood on the dock together.

Principles are like trees in open fields. We can know where we are and where to go. But the path we take is our own. What good is law today? We fight off rules like branches hitting us in the face, losing any sense of where we are supposed to be going and bleeding from illogical dictates that serve no one's purpose.

The sunlight of common sense shines high above us whenever principles control: What is right and reasonable, not the parsing of legal language, dominates the discussion. With the goal shining always before us, the need for lawyers fades along with the receding legal shadows. People understand what is expected of them. Law has lasting stature, as a beacon for common goals and a wise forum in times of trouble, and no longer meddles in our daily affairs. Law would be law again.

STEPPING OUT FROM LAW'S SHADOWS

Like prisoners in a dungeon too long, we want to get out, but the prospect frightens us. We have grown accustomed to a static system in which no one, including us, has to take responsibility. Our memory of anyone making decisions is so distant that we equate giving responsibility with anarchy. We have been led to believe that government should operate like an error-free machine. Like the bureaucrats we despise, all we think about is what might go wrong, not what might get done.

The cell doors open wide to the verdant fields of free choice. But we pause when the wardens of modern law begin their matter-of-fact description of life outside their control: Law will no longer provide the final answer; bureaucrats will make decisions; people will disagree; everything will depend. Uncertainty, they caution us, will descend upon society like the Dark Ages. We turn away from the opened door, and shuffle back to our places within the safety of the huge legal monument.

The fears that keep us quivering in law's shadows are, in fact, the rudiments of a strong society. Constant exposure to uncertainty and disagreement is critical to everything we value, like responsibility, individualism, and community.

Ridiculous, scoff the wardens of law: Everyone knows that unless law is set forth with certainty, society will break apart in fighting, especially, they tell us in portentous tones, in a society as diverse as ours. But their accepted wisdom is difficult to support by common experience. Tranquillity across the land is hardly the status quo; the trend line appears to point sharply in the other direction. The fights over "clear" rules are often marked by extreme bitterness — witness the parents who demand their children's "rights."

The effort to achieve social quiescence through clear rules, while plausible enough as a theory, has in fact infected the nation with a preoccupation with using law as a means to win: If the law is clear, we can fit ourselves into its words, and then — voilà — we get exactly what we want. But most services that a democratic society seeks to provide — decent education for all children, a practical and effective environmental law — are not win-or-lose propositions. Sensible results come out of discussion and negotiation, not from seizing technicalities and parsing legal language to achieve a victory. As a study of local regulation in Janesville, Wisconsin, concluded:

What the people in Janesville say they want is a spirit of accommodation in which the two parties, the regulated and regulator, try to work out a mutually acceptable solution to a common problem. What they get, they say, is an adversary relationship in which the regulators more often than not try to force something down their throats because it's written in a manual.

Human nature turns out to be more complicated than the idea that people will get along if only the rules are clear enough. Uncertainty, the ultimate evil that modern law seeks to eradicate, generally fosters cooperation, not the opposite. The contractors and the state officials rebuilding the Santa Monica freeway both had a lot to lose by being unreasonable. Humans are driven to be reasonable with each other because uncertainty puts both at risk. The "conflict" that modern law has preempted is what used to be known as give-and-take; as Professor Joel Handler has explained, it is the interaction that weaves the fabric of every strong community and healthy relationship.

But are we really willing, the wardens of law ask as we consider the exit again, to let bureaucrats loose without precise instructions? Law that is not crystal clear has to be interpreted by someone. Take your pick, they say, of whose thumb to be under — the rule of law, or the whim of a power-crazed bureaucrat?

We stop dead in our tracks. Fear of government authority, perhaps more than anything else, has kept us huddling in law's shadow. It's why we got into this tangle in the 1960s. We didn't trust government to do what we were asking it to do, so we decided to invent a modern legal system that would lay it all out in advance. We tied ourselves to legal millstones, like OSHA's four thousand rules, rather than run the risk of being told what to do by a civil service version of George III.

Thinking in extremes might be our national disease. We seem to believe a regulator is either bound by a clear rule or roams free with his sword unsheathed and a smirk on his face. But that isn't our choice. A bureaucrat's authority is what we define it to be. Having the discretion only to recommend, for example, isn't much power, but it's plenty effective if the bureaucrat has a valid point. The concept of having discretion itself implies constraint: "An official's discretion," legal philosopher Ronald Dworkin reminds us, does not mean "that he is free to decide without recourse to standards of sense and fairness."

Relaxing a little and letting regulators use their judgment is the only way to liberate our judgment. Discretion, it is vital to understand, works both ways. If the regulator has flexibility to interpret a general standard, so do we. We can think for ourselves. As the head of a large company said recently: "The majority of people will do right if they're given goals and left to get the job done. . . . Regulations telling us how long our ladders should be are not useful."

I can almost hear a swelling chorus of lawyers and bureaucrats chanting, "A government of laws, not of men." We don't trust bureaucrats. Who elected them? But we don't have an alternative; if there is no flexibility for the regulator, there is no flexibility for us. Creating rules without flexibility is just a version of central planning.

It is perhaps a hateful thought to give government officials a measure of discretion, but that's the only way for them to do anything, and the only way for us to know who to blame. Giving responsibility does not imply high confidence; as New Dealer Jim Landis noted, "We must take into account that government will be operated by men of average talent and average ability." The point is to put them on the spot. As Oliver Wendell Holmes suggested:

> When you get the dragon out of his cave into the plain and in the daylight, you can count his teeth and claws and see just what is his strength. The next step is either to kill him, or to tame him and make him a useful animal.

Taking responsibility was, of course, the basic premise of the republic. It's how we get accountability. In a study of two scandals involving fraudulent data, Christopher Stone found the "key actors were willing to prepare distortive documents; but they drew the line at putting their names on them." Like it or not, responsibility is the least dangerous system.

Responsibility is the last thing bureaucrats want. The head procurement officer of a New York agency, a dedicated public servant, bristled when we asked why he had to jump through all the hoops to award a straightforward contract. These procedures pose no hurdles, he said, if you know how to manage it; a contract sometimes can be awarded in as little as eighteen months. No other system, he stated firmly, would be acceptable, because fraud would be rampant. When we asked why fraud would be a problem in his agency, since he was the one making the decisions, he ended the interview.

Responsibility requires the attributes we used to value the most: effort and courage and leadership. Justice Cardozo put it this way:

> He must gather his wits, pluck up his courage, go forward one way or the other, and pray that he may be walking not into ambush, morass, and darkness, but into safety, the open spaces, and the light.

I can feel the ground shaking from millions of bureaucrats running in the opposite direction. They have come to believe that the only purpose of process is to protect them.

Seeing the glint of the American spirit in our eyes, the wardens of law don't bother to argue anymore, but are overheard to comment, as we head for daylight, that we may be back when we see how much work is required. They're right. Making judgments is hard, and some failures are inevitable. It's far easier to lounge around the basement TV room, hooting at any mistake or apparent unfairness. Balancing the needs of the greater good requires boring maturity, while cheering for special interests is great sport. The media will do their best to egg us on; headlines are more exciting when the needle oscillates wildly. All we have to do is fall for it, and demand instant legal fixes whenever a problem arises, and we'll be right back under law's shadow.

FINDING DEMOCRACY IN THE DAYLIGHT

"It's been thirty years," John Tuck, a former undersecretary of the Department of Energy, told me, "since I felt anyone has been excited about working in government." It has been about the same length of time since most Americans were excited about voting for anyone.

The reason is the same: No one has the ability to do anything. Democracy is as powerless as we are, because law has supplanted the decisions that made democracy important.

Why bother to elect anyone? Elected leaders can't exercise control over bureaucrats, because the law sets out almost everything that bureaucrats must do, and politicians quickly learn that no one's perspective means much in the dark shadow of all the accumulated rules and processes. They come to see their responsibility not as managing society but as piling up more legal stones.

We have invented a hybrid government form that achieves nearly perfect inertia. No one is in control. No one makes decisions. Only the massive weight of accumulated laws keeps everyone in check. "[T]he colonists challenged the king," Justice William Brennan noted in 1988. "Today citizens may find it impossible to know exactly who is responsible." The unfortunate side effect is that this modern system also crushes our goals and deadens our spirits. Samuel Francis, in *Beautiful Losers*, sounds our common lament:

> Today, almost the whole of American society encourages dependency and passivity. The result is an economy that does not work, a democracy that does not vote . . . a government that passes more and more laws, a people that is more and more lawless, and a culture that neither thinks nor feels except when and what it is told or tricked to think and feel.

Democracy has become a passive caretaker to a huge legal monument. After several decades of this menial duty, it exudes the dankness of someone who long ago gave up being vigorous. At Oxford they now talk about "the late period of American democracy."

As we venture out into the daylight and our eyes adjust to the open fields of free choice, however, the flag of democracy appears right alongside us, rippling in a fresh breeze. Trial and error, not a static monument, is what makes democracy thrive. Democracy was intended as a dynamic system, ever adjusting toward balance in a diverse society. The constant back and forth was not thought to be dangerous but protective; it makes vested power insecure and keeps society away from protracted disequilibrium.

People constantly making judgments is the breeze that drives out dank air and invigorates us. As conservative justice Antonin Scalia once explained, the "executive enfeebling measures" of modern law "do not specifically deter regulation. What they deter is change," including change by "dissolv[ing] the encrusted regulations of past decades." The observation of Justice Scalia sounds similar to that of the noted liberal and historian Arthur M. Schlesinger, Jr.:

> The problems are indeed complex. The answers are not in the back of anyone's books. . . . "It is common sense to take a method and try it," FDR said. If it fails, admit it frankly and try another. But above all try something.

Always trying something, or, as Tocqueville put it, having "the chance to make mistakes that can be retrieved," is the "great privilege" of Americans. More than anything else, he thought, it is what defines the American spirit. This approach "does not provide a people with the most skillful government, but it provides one that does much more: "[I]t spreads throughout the body a restless activity, superabundant force, an energy never found elsewhere."

Until the mid-twentieth century, no leader in our history ever thought that a fixed monument to logical uniformity was anything democracy should aspire to. Abraham Lincoln emphasized the need for government to be practical, and not to sacrifice needed goals in a vain pursuit of abstractions. Laws often have "some degree of inequality," Lincoln noted, but if this is unacceptable, then "we must discard all government." The unevenness that comes from making judgments fit the circumstances is just a part of life, and the resulting variability is no different from that occurring with decentralization, indeed federalism itself. Justice Cardozo suggested we strive for "a fair average of truth and wisdom." "The end," he said, "is laws' test and evidence of verity." Whatever works is good.

Relying on Ourselves

"The idea of law," Yale law professor Grant Gilmore cautioned in 1977, has been "ridiculously oversold." The rules, procedures, and rights smothering us are different aspects of a legal technique that promises a permanent fix for human frailty. Dictates are so precise that no one has the chance to think for himself. Procedural layers do away with individual responsibility. Rights are absolute so that choices among conflicting groups never need to be addressed, much less balanced. Law will be cleansed of human input. All tough choices, and indeed all choices, must be predetermined. As citizens and officials, we are allowed to argue during the lawmaking stage, but, day to day, we are precluded from making sense of the problems before us.

This legal experiment, we now learn for ourselves every time we encounter it, hasn't worked out. Modern law has not protected us from stupidity and caprice, but has made stupidity and caprice dominant features of our society. And because these dictates are supposed to be ironclad, we are prevented from doing anything about it. Our founders would wince; they knew that "the greatest menace to freedom," as former chief justice Earl Warren reminded us in 1972, "is an inert people."

No heroic vision is required for change. A quick glance in the mirror reveals the missing ingredient. That person ought to have a say in how things are done in his life. Decision making must be transferred, from words on a page back to people on the spot. This requires legal frameworks that are open, not open-and-shut.

One basic change in approach will get us going: We should stop looking to law to provide the final answer. Law should articulate goals, award subsidies, allocate presumptions, and provide mechanisms for resolving disagreements, but law should almost never provide the final answer. Life is too complex. Our public goals are too complex. Hard rules make sense only when protocol — as with the rules of a game or with speed limits — is more important than getting something done. When accomplishment or understanding is important, we have no choice: Law can't think, and so law must be entrusted to humans and they must take responsibility for their interpretation of it.

Accepting the imperfections and asymmetries of human nature is probably the bitterest pill for those schooled in the modern age. Just when we thought we were going to turn society into a perfectly calibrated machine of precise obligations and rights, somebody comes along and says people have to use their own two feet and a little judgment to get where they want. "We must spread the gospel," Justice Cardozo said in the 1920s, "that there is no gospel to spare us the pain of choosing at every step." Every generation has smart people who think they can figure everything out, once and for all. We happen to be the generation that fell for it.

Tocqueville, with his usual clairvoyance, suggested that when democracy fails, it would not die as Rome did, through invasions of the barbarians, but slowly: "If the lights that guide us ever go out they will fade little by little as if by their own accord." This would happen, he predicted, when we "lose sight of basic principles" and are "only able to make a clumsy and un-intelligent use of wise procedures no longer understood."

Conquering human nature was not the idea when our founders devised a new nation around the freedom of each human. Avoiding coercion by making law into a detailed manual only assures another form of coercion. Modernizing democracy with a huge legal monument crushes what may be one of democracy's most important qualities, continual trial and error. Curing the injustices of history and circumstance by awarding open-ended rights resurrects the specter of special legal privilege, a stature so inimical to a free society that it causes immediate and lasting discord.

We only meant to make society better. Law would lay everything out for us. But law cannot save us from ourselves. Waking up every morning, we have to go out and try to accomplish our goals and resolve disagreements by doing what we think is right. That energy and resourcefulness, not millions of legal cubicles, is what was great about America. Let judgment and personal conviction be important again. There is nothing unusual or frightening about it. Relying on ourselves is not, after all, a new ideology. It's just common sense.

ACKNOWLEDGMENTS

This book was made possible through the active interest and help of many friends and colleagues. Funding for initial research was provided by the William and Mary Greve Foundation and by the Arnold D. Frese Foundation, and I thank Tony Kiser and James S. Smith for their early encouragement. The Brookings Institution made available its research facilities and scholars, who provided an invaluable sounding board. The lawyers, librarians, and staff at Howard, Darby & Levin were continually helpful, and my partners were patient and encouraging.

Henry Reath lent his expertise and support at every stage. Kevin Fisher, Richard Boulware, and Philippa Dunne were thoughtful readers of numerous drafts, and Professor Richard Merrill at the University of Virginia provided detailed comments on certain sections. Dozens of friends and strangers graciously volunteered their time and resources; you know who you are, and I thank you all. My parents, John and Charlotte Howard, inspired and encouraged me.

Research assistance was vital, and David Nissenbaum and Rebecca Read Shanor each devoted a full year of resourceful support. Charles G. Salas and John Walsh, both at the Claremont Colleges, were important as sources. Judith Mogul, Jennifer Rothchild, Bill Ryan, Brad Sussner, and Sara Medina also did significant research. Professor Richard Bernstein provided useful initial thoughts on legal history.

My agent, Andrew Wylie, had the excellent judgment to arrange for me to work with Robert Loomis at Random House, who was always right on target.

AUTHOR'S NOTE ON SOURCES

The incidents described came from interviews in 1993 and 1994, and from accounts in newspapers and magazines, particularly *The New York Times, The Wall Street Journal, The Washington Post,* the *Chicago Tribune,* the *Los Angeles Times, New York Newsday, Forbes, Regulation,* and *The Washington Monthly.* Two interviewees' stories are told, at their request, with a pseudonym ("Jane O'Reilly" and "John Nesbit").

The literature on law and government is vast and dense. What follows is a bibliography that catalogs the principal sources that were relied upon, and also includes a fair sampling of other sources that I found helpful.

SELECTED BIBLIOGRAPHY

Ackerman, Bruce A., and Hassler, William T. *Clean Coal, Dirty Air.* New Haven: Yale University Press, 1981.

Alshuler, Albert W. "The Failure of Sentencing

Guidelines: A Plea for Less Aggregation." *University of Chicago Law Review*, Vol. 58 (1991), pp. 901–51.

Bardach, Eugene, and Kagan, Robert. *Going By the Book: The Problem of Regulatory Unreasonableness*. Philadelphia: Temple University Press, 1982.

Baum, Alice S., and Burnes, Donald W. *A Nation in Denial: The Truth About Homelessness*. Boulder: Westview Press, 1993.

Bennett, Linda L.M., and Bennett, Steven Earl. *Living with Leviathan: Americans Coming to Terms with Big Government*. Lawrence, Kans.: University Press of Kansas, 1990.

Berlin, Isaiah. *The Crooked Timber of Humanity*. New York: Alfred A. Knopf, 1990.

—. *Four Essays on Liberty*. Oxford: Oxford University Press, 1969.

Brennan, William J. "Reason, Passion, and 'The Progress of the Law,' " *Cardozo Law Review*, Vol. 10 (1988), pp. 3–23.

Breyer, Steven. *Breaking the Vicious Circle*. Cambridge: Harvard University Press, 1993.

Bryner, Gary C. *Bureaucratic Discretion: Law and Policy in Federal Regulatory Agencies*. New York: Pergamon Press, 1987.

Cardozo, Benjamin N. *The Growtb of the Law*. New Haven: Yale University Press, 1924.

—. *The Nature of the Judicial Process*. New Haven: Yale University Press, 1921.

Carter, Steven L. *The Culture of Disbelief*. New York: Basic Books, 1993.

—. *Reflections of an Affirmative Action Baby.* New York: Basic Books, 1991.

Chackerian, Richard, and Abcarian, Gilbert. *Bureaucratic Power in Society.* Chicago: Nelson-Hall, 1984.

Collins, Catherine, and Frantz, Douglas. *Teachers Talking out of School.* New York: Little, Brown, 1993.

Commager, Henry Steele. *The American Mind.* New Haven: Yale University Press, 1950.

Cose, Ellis. *The Rage of a Privileged Class.* New York: HarperCollins, 1993.

Cuomo, Mario M., and Holzer, Harold, eds. *Lincoln on Democracy.* New York: HarperCollins, 1990.

Davis, Kenneth Culp, and Pierce, Richard J., Jr. *Administrative Law Treatise,* 3d ed. Boston: Little, Brown, 1994.

Dehavenon, Anna Lou. "Charles Dickens Meets Franz Kafka: The Maladministration of New York's Public Assistance Programs." *New York University Review of Law and Social Change,* Vol. 17 (1989–90), pp. 231-55.

DiIulio, John J., Jr., ed. *Deregulating the Public Service.* Washington, D.C.: The Brookings Institution, 1994.

Diver, Colin S. "The Optimal Precision of Administrative Rules." *Yale Law Journal,* Vol. 93 (1983), pp. 65-109.

Donohue, John J., and Siegelman, Peter. "The Changing Nature of Employment Discrimination Litigation." *American Bar Foundation*

Working Paper #9021 (1990).

Dworkin, Ronald M. "Is Law a System of Rules?" reprinted in *Essays in Legal Philosophy*, edited by Robert S. Summers. Berkeley: University of California Press, 1976.

—. *Taking Rights Seriously*. Cambridge: Harvard University Press, 1977.

Ellickson, Robert C. *Order Without Law: How Neighbors Settle Disputes*. Cambridge: Harvard University Press, 1991.

Epstein, Richard A. *Forbidden Grounds: The Case Against Discrimination Laws*. Cambridge: Harvard University Press, 1992.

Etzioni, Amitai. *The Spirit of Community*. New York: Crown, 1993.

Feeley, Malcolm M. *The Process Is the Punishment: Handling Cases in a Lower Criminal Court*. New York: Russell Sage Foundation, 1992.

—, Piele, Philip K., Hollingsworth, Ellen Jane, and Clune, William H., III. *Schools and the Courts*, Vol. 2. Oregon: ERIC Clearinghouse on Educational Management, 1979.

Fitzhugh, William Michael, Jr. *The Effect of Due Process on the Provision of Social Services.* Doctoral dissertation, Columbia University, 1985.

Fox, Charles J., and Cochran, Clarke. "Discretionary Public Administration: Towards a Platonic Guardian Class," in *Images and Identities in Public Administration*, edited by Henry D. Cass. Newbury Park: Sage Publications, 1990.

Francis, Samuel. *Beautiful Losers: Essays on the*

Failure of American Conservatism. Columbia: University of Missouri Press, 1993.

Friendly, Henry J. "Some Kind of Hearing." *University of Pennsylvania Law Review*, Vol. 123 (1975), pp. 1267–1317.

Gilmore, Grant. *The Ages of American Law.* New Haven: Yale University Press, 1977.

Glendon, Mary A. *Rights Talk: The Impoverishment of Political Discourse.* New York: The Free Press, 1993.

Gore, Al. *Creating a Government That Works Better and Costs Less: Report of the National Performance Review,* rev. ed. New York: Penguin Books, 1993.

Gormley, William T., Jr. *Taming the Bureaucracy.* Princeton: Princeton University Press, 1989.

Grant, Gerald. "Children's Rights and Adult Confusions." *The Public Interest*, Vol. 69 (1982), pp. 83–99.

Green, Bruce A., ed. *Government Ethics Reform for the 1990s.* New York: Fordham University Press, 1991.

Greider, William. *Who Will Tell the People.* New York: Simon & Schuster, 1992.

Hall, Kermit. *The Magic Mirror: Law in American History.* New York: Oxford University Press, 1989.

Handler, Joel, F. *The Conditions of Discretion.* New York: Russell Sage Foundation, 1986.

—. "Continuing Relationships and the Administrative Process: Social Welfare." *Wisconsin Law Review* (1985), pp. 687–706.

—. *Law and the Search for Community.* Philadelphia: University of Pennsylvania Press, 1990.

Hart, H.L.A. *The Concept of Law.* London: Oxford University Press, 1961.

Havel, Vaclav. "The End of the Modern Era." *The New York Times* (editorial), March 1, 1992, sec. 4, p. 15.

—. "The New Measure of Man." *The New York Times* (editorial), July 8, 1994, sec. 4, p. 27.

Hayek, Friedrich A. *The Constitution of Liberty.* Chicago: The University Press, 1960.

Henderson, Gordon D. "Controlling Hyperlexis." *Tax Lawyer*, Vol. 43 (Fall 1989), pp. 177–86.

Hentoff, Nat. *Free Speech for Me — But Not for Thee: How the American Left and Right Relentlessly Censor Each Other.* New York: HarperCollins, 1992.

Holmes, Oliver Wendell, Jr. "The Path of the Law." *Harvard Law Review*, Vol. 61 (1897).

Hopkins, Thomas D. *The Costs of Federal Regulation.* National Chamber Foundation, 1992.

Horwitz, Morton J. *The Transformation of American Law, 1780–1860.* Cambridge: Harvard University Press, 1977.

—. *The Transformation of American Law: 1870–1960.* New York: Oxford University Press, 1992.

Huber, Peter W. *Liability: The Legal Revolution and Its Consequences.* New York: Basic Books, 1988.

Hughes, Robert. *The Culture of Complaint: The*

Fraying of America. Cambridge: Oxford University Press, 1993.

Isaac, Rael Jean, and Armat, Virginia C. "The Right to Be Crazy." *American Enterprise* (September/October, 1990), pp. 34–42.

Jacobs, James B. "Get out of Jail Free." *The City Journal,* Vol. 1, No. 4 (1991).

Jaffe, Louis L. "The Effective Limits of the Administrative Process: A Reevaluation." *Harvard Law Review,* Vol. 67 (1954), pp. 1105–35.

—. "Jim Landis and the Administrative Process." *Harvard Law Review,* Vol. 78 (1964), pp. 319–29.

Jencks, Christopher. *The Homeless.* Cambridge: Harvard University Press, 1994.

John F. Kennedy School of Government. "Building the Baltic." Cambridge: Harvard University Press, 1989.

—. "Employment Opportunity in the U.S. Department of Health, Labor and Commerce." Cambridge: Harvard University Press, 1979.

—. "Military Contracting: Getting out of the Business." Cambridge: Harvard University Press, 1989.

—. "Overcoming Police Corruption in Hong Kong." Cambridge: Harvard University Press, 1985.

Jones, A.H.M. *The Later Roman Empire, 284–602.* Norman: University of Oklahoma Press, 1964.

Jones, Harry. "The Rule of Law and the Welfare State." *Columbia Law Review,* Vol. 58 (February 1958), pp. 143–56.

Kagan, Robert A. "Adversarial Liberalism." *Journal of Policy Analysis and Management*, Vol. 10 (1991), pp. 369–406.

Katzmann, Robert A. *Institutional Disability: The Saga of Transportation Policy for the Disabled.* Washington, D.C.: The Brookings Institution, 1987.

Kaufman, Herbert. *Red Tape: Its Origins, Uses, and Abuses.* Washington, D.C.: The Brookings Institution, 1977.

Kaus, Robert. "How the People Lost Control." *The Washington Monthly* (July/August 1979).

Kelman, Steven. *Procurement and Public Management: The Fear of Discretion and the Quality of Government Performance.* Washington, D.C.: The American Enterprise Institute Press, 1990.

King, Martin Luther, Jr. *A Testament of Hope.* San Francisco: Harper & Row, 1986.

Kravchuck, Robert S. "Public Administration and the Rule of Law." *International Journal of Public Administration*, Vol. 14 (1991), pp. 265–301.

Lamb, H. Richard., ed. *The Homeless Mentally Ill: A Taskforce Report of the American Psychiatric Association.* Washington, D.C.: American Psychiatric Association, 1984.

Landis, James M. *The Administrative Process.* New Haven: Yale University Press, 1938.

Langbein, John H. "Torture and Plea Bargaining." *University of Chicago Law Review*, Vol. 46, No. 3 (1978), pp. 3–22.

Lemann, Nicholas. *The Promised Land.* New York: Alfred A. Knopf, 1991.

Light, Paul C. *Monitoring Government: Inspectors General and the Search for Accountability.* Washington, D.C.: The Brookings Institution, 1993.

Litan, Robert, and Nordhaus, William. *Reforming Federal Regulation.* New Haven: Yale University Press, 1983.

Manning, Bayless. "Hyperlexis and the Law of Conservation of Ambiguity: Thoughts on Section 385." *Tax Lawyer,* Vol. 36 (Fall 1982), pp. 9–15.

Mansbridge, Jane J. *Beyond Adversary Democracy.* New York: Basic Books, 1980.

Mashaw, Jerry L. "Prodelegation: Why Administrators Should Make Political Decisions." *Journal of Law, Economics and Organization,* Vol. 1, No. 1 (1985).

—, Merrill, Richard A., and Shane, Peter M. *Administrative Law, the American Public Law System.* St. Paul: West Publishing Co., 1992.

Matsuda, Mari, "Voices of America: Accent Discrimination Law, and a Jurisprudence for the Last Reconstruction." *Yale Law Journal,* Vol. 100 (1991), pp. 1329–1407.

McCarthy, Martha M. "Severely Disabled Children: Who Pays?" *Phi Delta Kappan* (September 1991), pp. 66–71.

McCraw, Thomas K. *Prophets of Regulation.* Cambridge, Mass.: Belknap Press, 1984.

McGarity, Thomas O. *Reinventing Rationality.* Cambridge: Cambridge University Press, 1991.

Mead, Lawrence M. *The New Politics of Poverty.* New York: Basic Books, 1992.

Melnick, R. Shep. *Between the Lines: Interpreting Welfare Rights*. Washington, D.C.: The Brookings Institution, 1994.

—. *Regulation and the Courts: The Case of the Clean Air Act*. Washington, D.C.: The Brookings Institution, 1983.

Melton, Gary B. "The Law Is a Good Thing (Psychology Is, Too)." *Law and Human Behavior*, Vol. 16, No. 4 (1992).

Mendeloff, John M. *The Dilemma of Toxic Substance Regulation: How Overregulation Causes Underregulation*. Cambridge: Massachusetts Institute of Technology Press, 1988.

Merton, Robert K., et al., eds. *Reader in Bureaucracy*. New York: The Free Press, 1952.

Mills, Nicolaus, ed. *Debating Affirmative Action*. New York: Delta Publishing, 1994.

Nagle, James F. *A History of Government Contracting*. Washington, D.C.: George Washington University, 1992.

Neal, David, and Kirp, David L. "The Allure of Legalization Reconsidered: The Case of Special Education." *Law and Contemporary Problems*, Vol. 48 (1985), pp. 63–87.

O'Quinn, Robert P. "The Americans With Disabilities Act: Time for Amendments." *Policy Analysis*. Washington, D.C.: Cato Institute, August 9, 1991.

Oakeschott, Michael. *On Human Conduct*. Cambridge: Oxford University Press, 1991.

—. "Reason and the Conduct of Political Life," in *Rationalism in Politics and Other Essays*. Indianapolis: Liberty Fund, 1991.

Olson, Walter K. *The Litigation Explosion.* New York: Penguin Books, 1991.

Osborne, David, and Gaebler, Ted. *Reinventing Government.* New York: Plume, 1993.

Parrish, Michael E. "The Depression, the New Deal, and the Legal Order." *American Law and the Constitutional Order*, edited by Lawrence M. Friedman and Harry N. Scheiber. Cambridge: Harvard University Press, 1988.

Posner, Richard A. *The Essential Holmes.* Chicago: The University of Chicago Press, 1992.

—. *The Problems of Jurisprudence.* Cambridge: Harvard University Press, 1990.

Preston, Larry M. *Freedom and the Organizational Republic.* New York: Walter de Gruyjer, 1992.

Reed, Leonard. "The Velvet Cage: The Life of a GS-15." *The Washington Monthly* (September 1979).

Reich, Charles. "Individual Rights and Social Welfare: The Emerging Legal Issues." *Yale Law Journal*, Vol. 74 (1965), pp. 1245–57.

—. "The New Property." *Yale Law Journal*, Vol. 73 (1964), pp. 733–87.

Renshon, Stanley A. "The Need for Personal Control in Political Life: Origins, Dynamics, and Implications," in *Choice and Perceived Control*, edited by Lawrence C. Perlmutter and Richard A. Monty. New York: Halsted Press, 1979.

—. *Psychological Needs and Political Behavior: A Theory of Personality and Political Efficacy.* New York: The Free Press, 1974.

Rosenblatt, Rand E. "Social Duties and the Problem of Rights in the American Welfare State," in *The Politics of Law*, edited by David Kairys. New York: Pantheon, 1992.

Rubin, Edward. "Law and Legislation in the Administrative State." *Columbia Law Review*, Vol. 89 (April 1989) pp. 369–451.

Scalia, Antonin. "Regulatory Reform — The Game Has Changed." *Regulation* (January/February 1981), pp. 9–13.

Schlesinger, Arthur M., Jr. *The Cycles of American History*. New York: Houghton Mifflin, 1987.

—. *The Disuniting of America*. Knoxville: Whittle Communications, 1991.

—. "A Time for Urgent Action." *Constitution* (Winter 1993).

Schoenbrod, David. "Goals Statutes or Rules Statutes: The Case of the Clean Air Act." *UCLA Law Review*, Vol. 30 (1983), p. 740.

Schuck, Peter H. "Legal Complexity: Some Causes, Consequences, and Curses." *Duke Law Journal*, Vol. 42 (1992), pp. 1–52.

Schwartz, Bernard, and Wade, H. W. R. *Legal Control of Government: Administrative Law in Britain and in the United States*. Oxford: Clarendon Press, 1972.

Schwarz, Jordan A. *The New Dealers: Power Politics in the Age of Roosevelt*. New York: Alfred A. Knopf, 1993.

Shapiro, Joseph P. *No Pity: People with Disabilities Forging a New Civil Rights Movement*. New York: Times Books, 1993.

Shapiro, Martin. "On Predicting the Future of Administrative Law." *Regulation* (May/June 1982), pp. 18–25.

Simon, William H. "The Invention and Reinvention of Welfare Rights." *Maryland Law Review,* Vol. 44 (1985), pp. 1–37.

—. "Rights and Redistribution in the Welfare State." *Stanford Law Review,* Vol. 38 (1986), p. 1431ff.

Sloan, Irving J., ed. *American Landmark Legislation.* New York: Oceana Publications, 1976.

State-City Commission on Integrity in Government. *Sovereign Commission Report.* New York: December 1986.

Stewart, Richard B. "The Reformation of Administrative Law." *Harvard Law Review,* Vol. 88 (1976), pp. 1667–1813.

—. "Regulation, Innovation, and Administrative Law." *California Law Review,* Vol. 69 (1981), pp. 1256–1377.

Sunstein, Cass R. *After the Rights Revolution.* Cambridge: Harvard University Press, 1990.

Sykes, Charles J. *A Nation of Victims.* New York: St. Martin's Press, 1992.

Toby, Jackson. "Crime in American Public Schools." *The Public Interest,* Vol. 58 (1980), p. 18.

Tocqueville, Alexis de. *Democracy in America,* edited by J. P. Mayer, translated by George Lawrence. New York: Harper & Row, 1969.

—. *The Old Regime and the French Revolution,*

translated by Stuart Gilbert. New York: Anchor Books, 1955.

Tribe, Laurence H. "Structural Due Process." *Harvard Civil Rights–Civil Liberties Law Review*, Vol. 10 (1975), pp. 269–321.

Vidmar, Neil, and Schuller, Regina A. "Individual Differences and the Pursuit of Legal Rights." *Law and Human Behavior*, Vol. 11, No. 4 (1987).

Vogel, David. "Cooperative Regulation: Environmental Protection in Great Britain." *The Public Interest*, No. 72 (1983), pp. 88–106.

Volcker, Paul A., Chairman. *Leadership for America: Rebuilding the Public Service*. Lexington, Mass.: Lexington Books, 1989.

Warren, Earl. *A Republic, If You Can Keep It*. New York: Quadrangle/The New York Times Book Co., 1972.

Weber, Max. *Economy and Society*, edited by Guenther Roth and Claus Wittich. Berkeley: University of California Press, 1978.

West, Cornel. "The Prospects for Democratic Politics: Reconstructing the Lippmann-Dewey Debate," in *Prophetic Thought in Postmodern Times: Beyond Eurocentrism and Multiculturalism*, Vol. 1. Monroe, Me.: Common Courage Press, 1993.

Wildavsky, Aaron. "The Secret of Safety Lies in Danger." *The Constitution and the Regulation of Society*, edited by Gary C. Bryner and Dennis L. Thompson. Provo, Utah: Brigham Young University, 1988.

Will, George F. *Statecraft as Soulcraft.* New York: Simon & Schuster, 1983.

Wilson, James Q. *Bureaucracy: What Government Agencies Do and Why They Do It.* New York: Basic Books, 1989.

—. *The Moral Sense.* New York: The Free Press, 1993.

Wilson, Woodrow. "The Study of Administration." *Political Science Quarterly,* Vol. 2 (June 1887), pp. 197–222.

Wiseman, Frederick. *Welfare* (documentary film). Zipporah Films, 1975.

Wynne, Edward. "What Are the Courts Doing to Our Children?" *The Public Interest,* Vol. 64 (Summer 1981), pp. 3–18.

Zirkel, Perry A. "Offensive Parents." *Phi Delta Kappan* (March 1992), pp. 572–75.

—. "Testing the Limits." *Phi Delta Kappan* (February 1990), pp. 490–92.

UNITED STATES GOVERNMENT PUBLICATIONS

Administrative Procedure Act: Legislative History. Washington, D.C.: Government Printing Office, 1946.

Department of Education. "National Excellence: A Case for Developing America's Talent." Office of Educational Research and Improvement. Washington, D.C.: Government Printing Office, October 1993.

Executive Office of the President, Office of Management and Budget. *Interagency Task Force Report on the Federal Contract Audit Process.* Washington, D.C.: Office of Management and Budget, December 3, 1992.

Executive Office of the President, Office of Management and Budget. *Regulatory Program of the United States, April 1, 1992–March 31, 1993.* Washington, D.C.: Government Printing Office, 1993.

General Accounting Office. *Performance Management: How Well Is the Government Dealing with Poor Performers?* Washington, D.C.: Government Printing Office, 1990.

House of Representatives. "The Civil Rights Act of 1991." *Hearings Before the Committee on Education and Labor,* 102d Congress, 1st Session, April 24 and May 17, 1991.

House of Representatives, Committee on Ways and Means. *1993 Green Book: Overview of Entitlement Programs.* Washington, D.C.: Government Printing Office, 1993.

House of Representatives Report No. 52. *The Federal Paperwork Jungle.* Washington, D.C.: Government Printing Office, 1965.

Report of the President's Committee on Administrative Management (Brownlow Report). Washington, D.C.: Government Printing Office, 1937.

Senate. "Implementation of the Paperwork Reduction Act of 1980." *Hearing Before the Subcommittee of the Committee on Small Business,*

264

101st Congress, 1st Session, September 7, 1989.
Senate Report No. 93–125, 93:1. "The Federal
  Paperwork Burden." Washington, D.C.: Gov-
  ernment Printing Office, 1973.

The employees of G.K. HALL hope you have enjoyed this Large Print book. All our Large Print titles are designed for easy reading, and all our books are made to last. Other G.K. Hall Large Print books are available at your library, through selected bookstores, or directly from us. For more information about current and upcoming titles, please call or mail your name and address to:

G.K. HALL
PO Box 159
Thorndike, Maine 04986
800/223-6121
207/948-2962